It's a
Guy
thing

the essential guide

HELPING GUYS
BECOME
MEN, HUSBANDS,
and FATHERS

John King

DESTINY IMAGE® PUBLISHERS, INC.
P.O. Box 310, Shippensburg, PA 17257-0310

*"Speaking to the Purposes of God for this
Generation and for the Generations to Come."*

This book and all other Destiny Image, Revival Press, MercyPlace, Fresh Bread, Destiny Image Fiction, and Treasure House books are available at Christian bookstores and distributors worldwide.

For a U.S. bookstore nearest you, call 1-800-722-6774.
For more information on foreign distributors, call 717-532-3040.
Or reach us on the Internet: **www.destinyimage.com**

ISBN 10: 0-7684-2371-6
ISBN 13: 978-0-7684-2371-6

For Worldwide Distribution, Printed in the U.S.A.
4 5 6 7 8 9 10 11 / 09 08 07

Dedication

To Beccy: For having the grace to live with a work in progress.
To Jessica, Noah, and Amy: Thanks for letting me experiment on you!

Acknowledgments

Thank you to the many men and many friends who have helped me on my journey.

- ❖ *Evelyn & Peter King*: When faced with a choice concerning my birth, they choose life. For that I am grateful.
- ❖ *Brain & Bobbie Houston*: Who taught us that the "terrible twos" don't have to be terrible.
- ❖ *Ian Woods & John Cannone*: Who helped save our marriage and guide our parenting.
- ❖ *Dr. Edwin Louis Cole*: Who gave me the framework for manhood in which I am still building my life.

Endorsements

When I think of men's ministry, I think of John King. IMN (International Men's Network) and *It's A Guy Thing* have brought a relevant biblical perspective to an age-old issue. I encourage every pastor, men's director, dad, husband, and *man* to read *It's A Guy Thing*. You will soon realize there is a ministry that is answering the questions you are asking.

Kile Bateman
Pastor Evangel Temple W.F.
Co-Pastor Dream Center Chicago

John King's book, *It's A Guy Thing* is a much needed guide for men of all ages: single, married, or married with children.

In this generation, the cry is, "Where are the fathers? Where are the godly men who do not abdicate their God-given calling?" Remember, God is a Father...a Husband. He has entrusted us men with a high and holy calling.

This book is written with wit, confrontation, and Holy Spirit-anointed common sense.

Grow up your boys to be men of God. Buy this book for your sons and encourage them to practice these principles and they will become successful, happy, and fulfilled men in order to affect this generation for God.

Apostle Emanuele Cannistraci
Founder of Apostolic Missions International

John King targets and hits the key issues in the role of being a man—a Christ-like man.

Accepting responsibility for a man's decisions, honoring God, honoring your wife, honoring your parents, and honoring the church are the foundation for being a man of God.

John King communicates the essence of being a true man of God. Not from theory, but from the practical experience of his life.

Wisdom is applied truth, and John King brings to all of us the wisdom of God so that it is practical, applicable, and memorable for all.

Read and apply the principles of *It's A Guy Thing*—you and those you love will be grateful for it.

Dr. John Harold Binkley, Jr.
Chairman, CEO
GW Equity, LLC.

Table of Contents

PART 2

RAISING KIDS

I CANNOT THINK OF

ANY NEED IN CHILDHOOD

AS STRONG AS THE NEED FOR

A FATHER'S PROTECTION.

Sigmund Freud

Preface

I wrote this book not with the onus of it being a literary master-piece but as a manual for men.

And I wrote it as a man to men with short chapters about specific topics of interest.

Men generally think this way. We want to get to the point. We want an answer to our question. And if we want to look it up later, we want to be able to find it quickly. So even after much editorial discussion, I have decided to keep it in this format.

So, men, enjoy it.

And ladies, excuse me—it is, after all, the men in your life I am trying to help.

John King

Introduction

He can empower dreams or destroy destinies. He can inspire people to reach the heights or confine them to life's deepest valleys. He can equip them for great things or leave a great hole in their hearts. He's a father: Daddy, Pa, the Old Man. He is Dad.

The fact that you've opened this book shows you're interested in becoming the best man, husband, and father you can be. Or perhaps you want to encourage your man to take on the fullness of a father's role. Or maybe you want to resolve issues with your own father. That's why we're here.

Fathers. Few subjects are as important, or as neglected. I'll share some astonishing research with you. You'll see the impact that fathers and fatherlessness have had on families and society.

It's a neglected subject because guys have never been keen to ask for help about how to be a dad. It's like asking for directions when we're driving—it's not a guy thing. Well, maybe that's not true—only stereotypical. I always ask for directions. I hate wasting time being lost.

That's how I approach life. That's how I approached discovering what it was to be a man and how I could be the best husband and, in later years, the best father.

I didn't know how, so I started to ask.

We are all looking for dad. We are all searching. We all want to connect. We all want to hear our dad say, "I love and accept you. I believe in who you are now and who you will become."

PART

1

Let's Get
Real

My Story

For as long as anyone knew or could remember, the men of my family had not been able to establish sound relationships between father and children, particularly between father and son. In fact, poor and broken relationships were all we'd known for at least four generations.

I have a great dad who tried really hard to do what he did. But he was 17 when Mom got pregnant and 18 when they got married. He was just a kid starting out with no concept of how to be a father. People face such difficult things in life and I think we judge them too harshly sometimes. People are amazing. Their ability to overcome, survive, and prosper is amazing.

So here was my Dad, a boy having a boy, and he just didn't know what to do. Therefore I grew up in an environment where my father didn't know what it was like to father effectively. I was a by-product of that. So when I became a husband and father, I realized there were a lot of issues to overcome. I'd come from generation after generation of King men who didn't know how to be a father or a husband.

I knew I had to break that pattern and live believing that the curse had been broken. I had to rebuild the walls of my mind, my will, and my emotions. In other words, I had to set about equipping myself to be a good husband and father.

That's when I started my search for the best wisdom around.

And that's why the following chapters are full of practical material I've seen work best in my life and in the people around me. Come on—leave behind everything that's held you back.

So here was my Dad, a boy having a boy, and he just didn't know what to do.

Our children are the ones who will live out the benefits of redeemed relationships. Our sons will live in a family where father and son are friends and lifelong companions.

Our daughters will be raised in an atmosphere of love, protection, security, and affirmation. They will have a sound, wholesome connection to their father, so when it comes time for them to marry, they will go looking for someone who will love them, respect them, honor them, care for them and support them in every endeavor.

This book isn't a cure-all. I don't have all the answers.

What I do have are lessons learned, observations made, and a determination to help as many men become what they want to be: good men, great husbands, and fantastic dads.

Let's begin the journey together.

Looking for Dad

We have a generation of boys, raised by women, who don't know how to be *men*. Have you noticed there's virtually no material out there on how to be a mother? It seems that moms just click into the role. Moms just seem to know when to hold you, when to cuddle you, what to say and what not to say. But dads...many of us find it difficult, if not impossible, to click with our kids.

That distance between fathers and their children is all too common. Maybe you've experienced the feeling that dad just doesn't seem to be there for you? Maybe he tries, but he's in a different place—far away physically or emotionally. Yet in your heart you know it's important to search for your dad, find him and reconcile with him—not only for you now, but also for your future.

It's one of our basic human needs. Adults often come to the point in their lives when they go on a search to find or discover who their father really is. Sometimes it happens after a time of wandering, or it comes out of a need for the security and reassurance only a father can give.

Whatever the reason to "go look for dad," it's a journey everyone should make. We get to discover the gifts of life and love shared between fathers and children—so wonderful, but so rarely understood or expressed.

There is a terrible impact on the life of a child when Dad is not around.

A father is like a compass for a child. A compass does two things: it shows you where you are headed and it gives your world orientation.

You take a father out of the life of a child and the child loses a great sense of where they are and who they may become.

Families Need Fathers

For at least two generations, the role of husband and father has been greatly devalued. The media, society, and even governments have denounced the role of fathers, and men in general, in our communities. Yet the impact of fatherlessness on our society is incredible.

Nearly 22 percent of American children live in a fatherless home.

Those kids make up:

- ❖ 63 percent of all youth suicides (Source: U.S. DHHS Bureau of the census).
- ❖ 70 percent of all juveniles sentenced to state-operated institutions (Source: U.S. Dept. of Justice Special Report, Sept. 1988).
- ❖ 71 percent of all high school dropouts (Source: National Principles Association Report on the State of High Schools).
- ❖ 75 percent of all young chemical-abuse patients (Source: Rainbows for all God`s Children).
- ❖ 80 percent of all drug users.
- ❖ 80 percent of anger-driven rapists (Source: Criminal Justice & Behaviour, Vol. 14, p. 403-26, 1978).
- ❖ 85 percent of all behavioral disorders (Source: Center for Disease Control).

❖ 85 percent of youths in prison (Source: Fulton Co. Georgia jail populations, Texas Dept. of Corrections, 1992).

❖ 90 percent of all homeless and runaway children.[1]

In Australia, when parents split up, the vast majority of children live with their mother. Ninety-six percent of the children under the age of 4 live with Mom. Eighty-nine percent of the 5 to 11 year olds do, too. From the ages of 12 to 17, 82 percent live with Mom.[2] That was in 1998. The same statistics bureau predicts that by 2020, a third of preschool children will be living with a single parent.

It's no wonder there are so many people who don't know what it is like to have a dad, or how to be one, don't know how to be a husband or what a husband should be like because they have never seen one!

Is fathering really so important? If the relationships between children and fathers are messed up, does that really make a difference in the world?

Let's break it down. If there's no dad in the house, or he is a non-participating member, the children are:

❖ 5 times more likely to commit suicide.

❖ 9 times more likely to end up in a state-operated institution.

❖ 9 times more likely to drop out of high school.

❖ 10 times more likely to abuse chemical substances.

❖ 14 times more likely to commit rape (this statistic applies to boys).

❖ 20 times more likely to have behavioral disorders.

❖ 20 times more likely to end up in prison.

❖ 32 times more likely to run away.

I think it's clear that when dads aren't around, the impact is incredible and generational. The effect of fatherlessness is a compelling reality. It is statistically frightening. And the impact on society is not going to go away—only recycle a tragic pattern.

Because fatherlessness affects everyone, our first task is to redefine the role of a father.

Endnotes

1. Dads4kids.com

2. Australian Bureau of Statistics—Marriages and Divorce.

"I've Got a Dad!"

John Cannone, a friend of mine, runs a church just outside Sydney, Australia. John is an avid outdoorsman. He thinks nothing of strapping a little tin boat to the roof of his car and taking his family into the Australian wilderness for a week of fishing. They take a tent, water, and no food! I'm talking about fishing for food. If they don't catch anything, they don't eat for a week. They always come home a little skinnier, but with great stories.

Like most young families, the Cannones were not particularly affluent in the early stages of their marriage. Not affluent, but rich. John's great wealth came from being a dad.

When the GameBoy craze went through school, everyone had one… except the Cannone boys. It wasn't just that the family couldn't afford it—they felt they didn't need it. The other kids had all the electronic gadgets…but many didn't have dads, only absent or divorced fathers.

The Cannone boys didn't envy the other kids their GameBoys. Amazingly, it was the other way round. The other young men were jealous of the Cannone lads, because they had a great relationship with their dad.

The other guys wanted to go along fishing, visit their house, and show off their new gadgets—all to be near the man who loved his boys and spent time with his family.

Flocking to Fathers

I see that all the time. Kids who don't have sound parenting at home love to hang around other kids who have good parents. They want to be part of a positive place that's full of love and affirmation. Kids will flock to an environment like that.

If you are creating a place of value and worth for your children, then your kids' friends will come flocking around as well. They want to be in an environment where they're affirmed.

Little kids of 4 and 5 will come and sit with me, because they hear me telling my daughter how important she is and how valuable she is. They want to hear that, too. They want to get in on the love.

That's prime dad territory: affirming children. No one does that better than Dad.

Not an Optional Extra

An optional extra. I think that's how a lot of dads view themselves—as a family accessory. They think their wives are the primary parent.

But it's just not the case. Dads are *not* optional extras.

We're vital—absolutely vital—in the process of raising kids. We're vital lovers and vital caregivers. We provide things that are totally different from what children get from their mothers.

We have to see the value in what we do. I don't think a lot of guys see the value in who they are and what they do.

As a dad you create your children's world! You make their world happen for them. If their world is inspiring, joyful, and filled with fun, light and excitement, then dad is playing a major role in establishing that. If it's a miserable, horrible, rotten place, then in large part the responsibility for that comes down to dad.

Dads Can Demolish Lives

Here's an experience that conveys the power of a father to create his child's world or to destroy it, even after childhood has been left far behind.

While in New Zealand preaching, I met a woman who had been in Christian ministry with her husband for many years. She told me she had the best father in the world. He was a prince—a Christian guy who loved God, his wife, and his kids. He was working hard to build a wealthy inheritance for his family. What a dad! He was doing all the right things.

Then suddenly he just divorced his wife and took off with another woman. The effect on his daughter was shattering. Even though she was in her 30s, with a marriage and life of her own, her world just crumbled.

She told me that her own marriage literally stopped. Everything closed down for them—their love life, their emotional life. She told me, "I don't believe in the dream any more. I've given up. If it happened to my mom, then it will happen to me! My parents had it all!"

She stood there saying this as her husband looked on desperately.

A dad has the power to shatter the lives of his children, even when they are 30-something. A dad can build worlds—and a dad can demolish them. That is the power a man has to affect and impact lives.

In one generation we have seen the world plummet into moral decline—so in one generation we can see the world rise.

In one generation the world has wallowed in perversion—in one generation we can see it embrace purity.

In one generation the family unit has been shattered—so in one generation marriage can be restored.

In one generation males have moved from "macho" to "Jell-O"—in one generation males can become men.

Embrace It, Don't Run From It!

Some political lobby groups have tried to marginalize and devalue fatherhood. But the value of a father to his family cannot be denied. A father is someone who animates his family by the spirit that's within him. If you're a dad, you're animating your children, reproducing after your own kind.

You didn't simply donate some DNA at conception. You are constantly animating your children. Whatever you are, that's what will be passed on to your children. It's the onus of every man who is a father. You can't run away from it. If you do, you'll simply animate your children with the abandonment and rejection that's in your spirit.

Don't even try to run from your responsibility. Embrace it. Embrace being a dad, because animating your children with the good things in your spirit is the greatest work on earth a man can ever do.

SETTING SHANNON FREE

I met "Shannon" at a seminar in Australia. I was teaching on the issue of fatherlessness. The presentation was all about reconciliation and forgiveness. How strongly people desire to forgive their fathers, because forgiveness is the gateway to a decent relationship with dad—and that's what people crave.

At the end of the service that night, Shannon came up with her foster mom. Ten years old, cute, with pigtails and big, round glasses—fragile, with a broken heart. Shannon came up and wanted to hug me. Then, in a little shaky voice, she started to tell me her story, one that still brings me to tears.

She told me about how when she was younger her father and mother tried to murder her. There were other terrible things, too. Her parents used her in satanic sex rituals. As she told her story to me, she stared tearlessly ahead. She had been betrayed by her father and violated by her mother.

She looked at me and said, "I can never forgive my dad." Yet through the strong hatred Shannon had for her parents, there was a yearning to forgive them. She desperately wanted a dad, so we sat and talked a little while longer.

I shared my story; told her things I had not told others; told her about what people had done to me when I was a little boy. I talked about how hard it had been and how it will take a lifetime to get over, but that one day, with God's help, she will feel better. She sat for the longest time and then slowly turned to her foster mom and said, "Mom, would it be all right if I came to church tonight and asked God to forgive my dad?"

That night I saw Shannon do something that little girls just don't do when they've been so hopelessly betrayed by their fathers: she danced and sang for the first time in her life, and hugged. She hugged me probably 20 times that night and hung on until my neck hurt.

EARLY IN MY CAREER, I THOUGHT
I WAS JUST AN ACCESSORY IN MY
CHILDREN'S LIVES...MY PARTNER'S
HELPMATE IN PARENTING.

Steve Biddulph

Turn This World Around

If enough men decide they're going to be fathers to their families, we can turn this world around. All it will take is a generation that says, "I will father the children. I may be fatherless myself, but that doesn't matter. I'm going to be a father to the next generation." I believe that's the cry of this generation, the generation of men who will rise to become fathers.

If we as dads take responsibility, we can totally transform our society. The statement "The hand that rocks the cradle rules the world" does not appear to be true. We can see from the statistics that it is the *father* who frames the generation. A father has so much power. A father has the power to define a child's life. We can make our children's lives either heaven or hell. If we are loving, consistent, involved dads, we have the power to turn a whole generation around.

You've seen that your family needs you. Now let's explore the amazing power you have to fulfill that need.

Fatherhood — A Gift From Dad

THE GIVING—CORRECTION, PROTECTION, DIRECTION

Above all, there are three things a father should give to his family: correction, protection and direction. When these gifts are absent, other factors step into place—like street gangs that are so prevalent in cities today. They give kids the three things a dad is supposed to provide.

A gang delivers correction, protection, and direction to young people. It provides parameters, security, and a sense of belonging—everything that a child is supposed to get from a family, in particular, a father.

Most gang members come from homes where there is a mother but no father. The issue isn't socio-economic, political, or cultural. It's all about families and fathers. If society wants to address the issue of gangs, legislation isn't the answer. Fathering is the answer. If a dad isn't giving a sense of value and a sense of leadership, then someone else will. Let's hope it's a church and not a gang. Best of all, though, it would be Dad.

A "father" doesn't necessarily have to be a child's biological parent. A father takes the time to sit down and bring correction to the attitudes and actions of a child. He takes responsibility to ensure that they are heading in the right direction to fulfill their own personal destiny.

Protection isn't the macho concept of beating up the bad guys. It might be as simple as protecting someone from the wrong influences, or steering them from destructive relationships and helping them make productive ones.

It's not even an age thing. It's perfectly possible for you to father someone who is older than you. You just have to have an attitude and desire to reach out to someone, to love them and care for them, a desire to see them go on to greatness. Fatherhood is as much about attitude as biology. In fact, some of the worst dads I have met have been biological fathers living in the family home—but they're not active in any way in shaping or forming a family life. They are ghosts, shadows of the men they should be. They're wisps that blow in and out of the family home without tangibly touching anyone's life.

THE DOING—BELIEVE, DREAM, SUPPORT

There are three things a father is supposed to do for his family: believe in them, dream with them, and support them.

I think our homes should be dream factories. Family is a place where anything can happen! Octopuses can be lime green, elephants are yellow with four ears, little boys are Superman, and little girls, Wonder Woman.

Often at school a child is told what they can*not* do. In fact, many people's entire lives are limited by the negativity they experienced at school. Most people never achieve their dreams and a lot of them go on to impose their negative worldview on the people around them.

Well, our job as dads is the complete opposite. We should be telling our children what they *can* do: "Yes! You can be a brain surgeon, a member of a band, a business woman, a preacher, a fashion model, and a world-renowned author!" (all in the same breath, as the moods change). Homes have to be an environment for dreams. It is a father who creates that environment. Fathers have a great capacity to sow faith into their kids. You need to believe in your kids!

As practical men, we are tempted to rationalize things for our kids, to bring a reality check when our kids start exploring impossible dreams and visions. Dad, a wet blanket? This isn't a dad's job, surely. Isn't the world enough of a wet blanket to our children's hopes and dreams? Dad should just believe in his kids, whatever they want to do. Life will temper their passion; you should fuel it!

Believe and support whatever they want to try. How much does it really cost you? Suppose your child chooses to try a different sport every year. Dad should just believe in his kids, whatever they want to do. Golf one year, tennis the next, football the year after that. Kids go through these things, and yes, it does cost money. But what does a set of second-hand golf clubs cost, really? What does a football cost? A used tennis racquet?

Dad should just believe in his kids, whatever they want to do.

Between the ages of 14 and 17, if your child decides they are going to become a world champ at a different sport every 12 months, it will really only cost you a few hundred dollars to enable them to pursue their dream, to support them, and believe in them. What if all of a sudden your kid drops the sport and decides to become a great singer or a TV commentator? That's fine. It's not a problem. They don't have to achieve their dream; they are just looking for the dream that will fit them.

They just have to know that Dad believes in them. The cost of that sports equipment or battered old guitar is actually an investment in the health of their soul and in your relationship with them. Support your kids in all their endeavors. That's what a dad does with his kids—dreams with them, believes in them, supports them.

Oh yeah, but make them complete the year! That teaches them to honor their commitments. It enforces consistency and self-discipline.

The Being—Stewardship, Leadership, Relationship

A father brings three things out of his being and offers them freely to his family: stewardship, leadership, and relationship.

Stewardship—over finances, relationships, future, direction, dreams as a family, and even our performance as parents.

I'm constantly talking with Beccy about our relationship with our kids. We discuss how we can enhance it and become better parents. We have constant dialogue. This is me being a father: taking stewardship over the relationships in the family, helping my wife be a better mom, being teachable and open myself, and hearing from her about how I can improve as a dad.

A father brings leadership, too. A father sets the direction of the family. This is not something you can opt out of, for if you don't set the family's direction, it won't really have one. Nature abhors a vacuum. If you don't give leadership and you abdicate your responsibility, someone else will have to fill it. Your wife will have to carry the burden alone. Television, movies, and your children's school friends will become the strongest influences in their lives.

Finally, fathers bring relationship. Does that seem odd, knowing that women are naturally far more relational than men? Yes, women are, but men need to take responsibility for this because we set the tone of the family.

We can make wonderful relationships happen in our family, simply by deciding that's the way it's going to be. It's the power of choice. It's the power of a God-given position of responsibility and authority.

Your Family Owns You

I've been talking about the power of fathers, but power is always tied to purpose. Fathers have a choice: putting their power to positive impact or to negative purpose.

It starts with the realization that as fathers we are right at the bottom of the list in terms of personal rights. My personal view is that men own nothing.

You as a man are called to steward everything, but you don't own anything.

Your God owns you. Your children own you. Your wife owns you. You as a man are called to steward everything, but you don't own anything. You've been given a wonderful gift from God. It's called your family. We will be held accountable for how we look after that gift. On Judgment Day a man is not only judged on the conduct of his own life but also on the conduct of his wife and children.

Are you with me? I'm saying that our family gets to own us. We get to steward them. That makes us the servant of all.

I was once verbally attacked by a woman because she took offense at the term "my wife Beccy." She said it made Beccy sound like my property. Let me put it simply: my wife owns me and I own my wife. I am her property, she is mine!

My life is lived serving Beccy and her life is lived serving me. This is not just how marriage was designed; it's the only way a marriage can succeed! The only way two can become one flesh is if we lose half of ourselves. I get rid of the worst of me and she gets rid of the worst of her, *leaving the best of each other*—two selfless people living to love and serve each other. Does that sound impossible? It's not—and it should be our end goal, working a lifetime to achieve. Why marriages collapse is because two broken people get married and spend the years lusting and getting, not loving and giving.

I'm not saying a guy does not have a life of his own or that he can't do sports, watch the game, or work passionately at his career. But what I do want to do is buy back a balance. Our family is *our life*; it is an extension of us, not something separate from us. It is not something we occasionally attend to, but something we continually live for.

LEADERS ARE PREPARED TO SERVE

You're only a leader to the degree you're prepared to serve. If you want to be head of your home, you have to be prepared to serve in your home.

That doesn't mean you're a doormat. I said "serve," not "slave." It's a matter of rebalancing your priorities. In my family, I get my own time, I get my own space, but...I cannot afford to come home and be miserable and grumpy.

You come home. Your children reach for you. They smile at you. They hug you. They want to talk about their day. They might get snot on you when they're young. Tears come when they're older. They don't understand about male "cave time," and they shouldn't have to. This is what I mean by being owned. You come home and you're there to support your wife. You're there to reinforce what she's had to do during the day. You're there to support her in the decisions that were made and executed.

So on the one hand, as men, our view of leadership in the family does have to be strong and visionary. But there's this other side to being a leader, too—servant leadership. You can only lead by serving your family.

This is where so many men are stuck. They can't understand why the woman in their life isn't willing to submit to or respect their leadership. Primarily it's because the man hasn't activated the servant side of his leadership position. I've never met a woman who had a problem submitting to a man who was prepared to serve her.

A man needs space, time to be alone. It's part of the male character that we need a study, a den, a shed, or a beach where we can walk and get our headspace. Watching cartoons serves the same function. I understand that. We are not wired like women. But such time should not always be at the expense of family. *We must make room in our life for our family.*

IF YOU HAVE NEVER

BEEN HATED BY YOUR

CHILDREN YOU HAVE

NEVER BEEN A PARENT.

Bette Davis

Go Ahead, Make Their Day

I get a rush out of being the center of my children's world. I love being able to walk into a room and make their day. It's like walking onto the sports field in front of the fans. I love the feeling that I have to be in top form, because I have a chance to bring a smile to my children's faces. When Daddy comes home, the world just lights up for them. They want Daddy to come home.

Include Them in Your World

For me, 7 A.M. on Saturday morning at a café with a coffee and the newspaper is a beautiful space in the world. No one's around; just me, my coffee, and my newspaper. Every now and again, take one of your children with you. Include them in your world. Not necessarily all times, but some of the times. Kids will do what you want to do. If Daddy wants to go for a walk on the beach, they want to come along. If Daddy goes for a drive in the car, they want to go along. If Daddy watches football, they want to watch. They just want to be with Dad.

That's the power and joy of being your family's servant.

There is a myth that children want *quality* time. No they don't. They want *quantity*. As much as you've got, they want!

There is a pressure that you have to spend a lot of money taking your children somewhere to create memories. This is totally untrue.

My wife's two fondest memories of times with her father: When she was 10 years of age he let her help him with a house renovation; then at age 14 one Saturday morning he said, "You want to go for a drive?" They took off together. Cost: $20 for fuel. Impact: priceless.

A Hero, Not an Icon

There's a time in every dad's life when he stops being Superman. It's usually about the same time that Santa Claus stops being real. That's a natural part of life. Dad stops being an icon and becomes a hero. Icons are false, gaudy, and shallow.

A hero has longevity. A hero doesn't fade. A hero isn't tainted. Superstars are easily tarnished, but people will overlook the falls and failings of a hero.

As dads we don't need to be superstars; we need to be heroes. A superstar dad is there for the big flashy gestures, the extravagant gifts. A hero dad is there for the small and consistent things that speak of real character.

Dads love being heroes. That's great, because kids need heroes. I love being the hero dad. I am the invincible, all-knowing, spider-killing, fixer-upper of toys, and replacer of batteries. I make the dark go away. I make the bogeyman hide. I check for monsters under the bed. I am known throughout the domain of my reach simply as "The Man"!

But I catch myself trying so hard to be the perfect man my little girl thinks I am. What I know, though, is that I'm flawed. When I hear the scream, "I hate spiders!" I know I have to race in there with my cape on and kill every one of them. We love that affirmation we get from our kids. But a man never feels entirely worthy of the worship in a child's eyes. He's never quite the icon his daughter thinks he is, never quite the man his son believes him to be—and this worries him.

So he works too hard to try to smooth the rough places and tries too hard to make amends. We must relax and realize that even with our failings, if we love our children, we'll stay heroes... even if we eventually have to retire the superhero suit.

PARTICIPATION, NOT PROFICIENCY

Knowing that your kids want to idolize you, what if you can't do some of the things they expect of a superhero? They may expect you to play world-class soccer or major league football, for instance.

Don't be intimidated. If you happen to be utterly hopeless with ball skills, it's enough just to get out in the backyard and watch them kick or toss a ball. Take them to see a soccer game or football game. It's just best to be with them. It's not about proficiency; it's about *participation*. It's about your being secure at being a hero and not needing to be a superhero.

Fathers, Not Coaches

A "coach" is a highly respected model in sports, but also increasingly so in business, politics, and church life. At pastors' conferences and business leadership seminars we are being encouraged to find a personal coach or to coach others. People are paying their personal or life coaches big dollars to help them perform and achieve their goals. There is nothing wrong with that in some areas of life but it's not what is needed in family life.

There are huge differences between the role of father and coach. A father is not the family coach. There is no shortage of coaches or teachers in life—that is, people who will tell you how to live it, not walk with you through it.

Children do not need sideline coaches; they need active participants in the game of life. They need fathers, not coaches.

Here are some differences between the attitudes of a father and a casual coach:

A coach is paid for what he does.
A father loves what he does.

A coach is a professional pastor.
A father is a dedicated discipler.

A coach has an occupation.
A father has a lifestyle.

A coach selects you.
A father gave life to you.

A coach will drop you from
the side if you don't cut it.
A father will never leave
you or forsake you.

A coach will select you
based on performance.
A father will love you in
spite of performance.

A coach will change teams.
A father heads up the team.

A coach is in it for the season.
A father is in it for the long haul.

A coach yells from the sideline.
A father cries in the locker room.

A coach is responsible until
the end of the season.
A father is responsible for a lifetime.

A coach prepares players for a game.
A father prepares a child for life.

Many of us have settled for the term "coach" because we are uncomfortable with our experience with fathers. For me, that is not a good enough reason to settle for second best. I want to be the best and I want the best for my life. I would rather struggle, fight, and redefine "father" than settle for the detached concept of "coach."

I WATCHED A SMALL MAN WITH THICK CALLUSES ON BOTH HANDS WORK 15 AND 16 HOURS A DAY. I SAW HIM ONCE LITERALLY BLEED FROM THE BOTTOMS OF HIS FEET, A MAN WHO CAME HERE UNEDUCATED, ALONE, UNABLE TO SPEAK THE LANGUAGE, WHO TAUGHT ME ALL I NEEDED TO KNOW ABOUT FAITH AND HARD WORK BY THE SIMPLE ELOQUENCE OF HIS EXAMPLE.

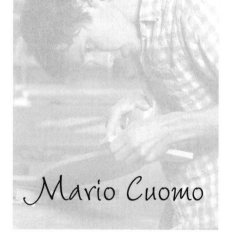

Mario Cuomo

ONE FATHER IS MORE

THAN A HUNDRED

SCHOOLMASTERS.

English Proverb

Fatherhood — Not a Spectator Sport

The family unit was designed to be the center of a man's world, not an annex. Even if time is short, make it count with your kids. Spend as much time with them as you can. Even if it's just a little time, it's still a start. Turn off the phone. Turn off the TV. Make your children aware that for the next while they are the most important people in your world.

The best way to make sure you have time for your kids is to actively schedule them into your schedule. Allocate time for your children. You can tell what a man loves by looking at his daily schedule and his credit card statement. Where we put our time, talent, and treasure reflects where our heart is.

ENGAGE!

Don't let the soccer coach teach your kid how to kick a ball. Get involved.

I know a lot of guys think they're doing the father thing just by sharing the same address as their children; they think that somehow (maybe it's magic?) just being an adult male in the family is enough.

It's not. This was brought home to me very clearly with survey results by popular youth speaker Josh McDowell. Josh looked at the emotional wholeness of children in two different types of families: two-parent families with a passive, uninvolved dad; and families with an actively involved single parent.

Josh found that children with a passive dad are actually worse off than if they have a single parent who is actively involved! Hear me, guys. For all the statistics about the impact of fatherlessness, if a father is just going to be a spectator in his child's life, it's actually detrimental! Children need you to be actively involved in their lives. Fatherlessness is not only absence *from* the family but also absence of concern and involvement *with* the family.

That survey is so earth-shaking because it means that the old idea about "staying together for the sake of the children" is irrelevant. It's not good enough to stay together just for the kids if you're going to ignore them. You have to engage with your children.

Engaging is not hard work; it's just an attitude. It just means taking the time to listen to your children about how they cleaned their teeth or what they did at college, or to listen to a song by a band you've never heard of. A lot of men get tense or even fly off the handle if interrupted by their children. But really, it just takes 30 seconds to celebrate with them as they experience life.

Celebrate with your son or daughter for cleaning their teeth...or making waffles...or working the computer, or earning an A, or experiencing a rush of independence—they want to share their lives with you.

Engagement is about all the small things—a whole series of small moments rather than large landmark events. It's the little things that make the difference.

Engaging is not hard work; it's just an attitude.

I learned this as a personal lesson when Jessica, our eldest daughter, was 5 years old and I started taking her for dates about once a month.

Sometimes we'd go for a drive, to McDonald's, a coffee shop, or a playground. This is what would happen: I'd hop in the car, drive for five or 10 minutes, place a bunch of phone calls while she was playing, drive with her to a coffee shop, place another bunch of phone calls, then drive her home thinking I'd had a really good time with her and I'd done my fatherly thing for the month.

Then one day we hopped in the car together and she said, "Daddy, can you please not turn on the phone while we're out? I just want to talk with you." Whoa! I'd been thinking I'd been doing a great job of blocking out a whole hour for her, but I hadn't. Twenty minutes of un-divided attention—that was what my child wanted from me.

It seems like we've lost a lot of the satisfaction of parenting. These days, people just don't seem to enjoy being moms and dads. There doesn't seem to be the time to go for a walk on the beach with the kids because there are too many other things to do. We're so overextended and over-leveraged in our lives that there's no room for the simple, no room for the important. We're too busy doing the spectacular to en-gage in the significant. We become spectators of our children's growth, not participants in it.

If you've been a spectator dad up to this point, you can become ac-tively involved *today*. You really just need to start. Depending on which report you read, they say that statistically the average Ameri-can father spends between 48 seconds and 2? minutes a day in real interactive time with their children. So if you make an effort to ex-pand that to 15 or 20 minutes a day, all of a sudden you're doing 10 times better than the national average!

Make a start and the kids will take care of the rest. Kids are addic-tive! You'll get hooked. Once you start spending that time with them—consistent time—you'll start to fall in love with your kids. Guys fall out of love, or forget what it is to love their children, be-cause there's so much going on in the "providing," "carving out," and "conquering" departments. Our families become forgotten, so any starting point is a good starting point.

Personally, I try to schedule the first hour after I come home for my family.

For the first 10 minutes I sit down with my wife and we share about our day. This produces a couple of very positive results. It shows her I love her and am interested in her and her day. It also models effective ongoing communication between husband and wife to my children. It shows them that my wife is the most important person in my life.

After that, it's time for the kids.

Any working guy knows that the first hour at home is not necessar-ily the best time. Your head is still spinning from the day. I might suc-ceed three out of five days, or five out of five, then the next week just one day out of five. But because it's there in my mind, it happens. Schedule in some blocks of time for your kids and protect those blocks with discipline. Once I get that hour done, if I need to hit the books, make phone calls, or finalize projects, I can, with a clear con-science and a supportive wife.

Quality Versus Quantity

We've had guilt-free chocolate and guilt-free ice-cream, so it's no surprise that there's been a big move toward the notion of guilt-free parenting. This is the basis for the whole "quality time versus quantity time" debate.

When I spoke about allocating an hour a day for my kids, I was talking only about the undivided, totally devoted time—the quality time. But kids need a lot more than that. Quality time is not enough. My experience is that kids want as much time with you as they can get. They are fully *quantity time* animals. They'll take 24/7 if they can get it.

Well, they can't get it, but they do need more than just the quality time. They need a mixture of quality and quantity. Not all the quantity has to be one-on-one quality, but you have to be prepared to share your life with your kids.

Kids need more than quality time. Share your life with your kids; don't make them learn from scratch.

GIVE IT ALL YOU'VE GOT

In this generation there are a lot of dads who don't feel they have much to give their kids. Some dads think they don't have enough money to be great fathers, because there's so much pressure on parents regarding materialism.

But if a dad wants to be ahead—directly or indirectly—of the crowd, it's really very easy. Over the past two generations in the Western world, up to 75 percent of people come from broken and dysfunctional families. So if you, as a father, want to put your children ahead of the vast majority of the population, all you have to do is love your children's mother and actively love your kids and interact with them. That simple combination will put you far ahead of the game. Compared to most guys, you can be a winner as a dad simply by being there and engaged in the moment.

Adjusting the EQ

We're all familiar with Intelligence Quotient (IQ), but Daniel Goldman has researched another aspect of intelligence, which he calls your Emotional Quotient (EQ).

IQ is about your ability to analyze bits and pieces. It's the way you think, the logical side of your brain.

EQ rates your ability to perform as a complete being.

Goldman's research suggests:

- ❖ If you have a low EQ, you need a high IQ to succeed in life.
- ❖ If you have a high EQ, you only need an average IQ to succeed.
- ❖ IQ is the result of genetics; EQ is the result of life's experiences.
- ❖ Your parents gave you both.

That means virtually any man can succeed as a father—if he's committed to emotionally interacting with his family. Financially, he might not be able to give his kids a lot, but the bucks don't come close to making the same impact on a child's life as a caring, engaged dad. By loving the kids and loving their mother, a man becomes one of the "Peak Parenting Performers" of our time. White collar or blue, it comes down to the EQ.

Certainly, you don't need a high IQ to spot the benefits of giving your children quality *and* quantity time. As a dad you give your children a sense of security about who they are. If my little girls get kisses every morning and every night, if they get cuddles and time with Dad, then their world is complete and whole.

Without that constant interaction, Dad is just a shadow in the background. As a result, children become insecure. They start misbehaving, trying to get the attention and affection they crave from their father.

As a father you wield immense power—either the power to have an adverse and negative effect on your children's lives which takes no time at all, or the power to positively fashion your children's world, their characters, and their behavior...and this does take time. Not quality time *versus* quantity time, but plenty of both.

Father — More Than a Friend

What Bette Davis was getting at when she said, "If you have never been hated by your children you have never been a parent" is the unavoidable fact that you *will* have conflict with your children. Remember that you are supposed to be the parent.

If there's a character issue with your children, you're supposed to handle it. It's good for your children to have a friend, but what they really need is a father.

At a men's event where I was speaking, a man came up to me and told me about his relationship with his son. He was very much in the "friend" mode with his eldest and said that his son had just moved in with his girlfriend. The son quit his job and the debts were mounting. His life was going nowhere as he got more and more tied up in activities and actions that weren't compatible with a successful life. His future and his current friendship looked disastrous.

This dad turned to me and said, "You know, I'm just trying to be his friend through all this." From me he wanted affirmation; what he got was confrontation.

"Let's talk about that," I replied. "What do you actually think about the life choices your boy is making?"

"I think it's really unfortunate," said this dad. "It's his circle of friends. This lady's not taking him where he needs to go. He has stopped his trade as a carpenter 12 months before its completion.

He has compromised his faith. He is such a bright lad with so much potential."

"So you're feeling disappointed."

"Yeah."

"Have you ever expressed those thoughts to him?"

"Well, no, because I don't want to lose him as a friend. I want to be there for him."

"There are times," I replied, "when you have to stop being a friend so you can be a father. Your son doesn't need another friend. He has lots of friends who are encouraging him to live this current lifestyle, but he has no one who is speaking into his life saying, 'Hey, are you aware there are consequences to your actions?'

"My advice to you is to take your son out and sit him down and talk to him. Look him square in the eye and say, 'I love you, son, but today I'm not talking to you as a friend but as a father. I want to outline to you where your current lifestyle is going to take you and what the consequences will be.'

"Don't lose your cool, don't get overemotional. Even try to stay detached. But clearly outline what the consequences of his current lifestyle will be."

The guy looked at me very soulfully. He'd always thought that being a friend to his son was the best mark of a father. He dropped his gaze and just stood there.

BEING MALE IS A MATTER
OF BIRTH. BEING A MAN IS
A MATTER OF CHOICE.

Ben Kinslow

Responsible for Responsibility

The next week was going to be tough for that man. His son wasn't going to enjoy hearing the hard truth from his dad. He'd probably react strongly to it, too, after having a father who had been such a compliant mate for so long. But it was vital that this dad explain the future for his son. It was his personal responsibility as a father.

I told him, "Once you've spoken the truth to your son, you've taken the onus off yourself. You will have placed the responsibility on your son. But if you're just observing him and not warning him, then you'll be accountable for the outcome of his life. The blood will actually be on your hands."

This is real maturity—the acceptance of this kind of responsibility. Not just responsibility for your own actions but also for your family's. Being a dad means taking it up a level and accepting responsibility for the lives of the people you love.

If you see your child doing an inappropriate thing or heading in an inappropriate direction, your responsibility is to make them aware of the consequences of their actions. This places the responsibility where it needs to be—with them. It is part of the process of growing our children to maturity.

In this way a man never stops being a dad. That's why this man was still responsible for speaking into his son's life, even though this young man was 22 years of age.

My children will have plenty of friends, but only one dad. It's the privilege and responsibility of every father to be so much more than a friend to his children.

Four Steps to Fatherhood

There are four practical steps to becoming a dad. We'll look at them in more detail in the next sections, but here, in brief, is the four-step journey toward becoming a dad.

1. TAKE RESPONSIBILITY

   Men have been struggling with this ever since Adam was convicted in the "fruit-gate" scandal. You know the line, "The woman made me do it." But as men you must take responsibility for your life, your actions, and your family.

2. SAY YOU'RE SORRY

   Learn the power of an awesome five-letter word—sorry.

3. ASK FOR FORGIVENESS

   You've held bitterness and unforgiveness toward the family you had or the family you didn't. That's human nature. That's part of your brokenness. Ask their forgiveness. Learn to receive and give forgiveness.

4. BREAK THE CYCLE

   You need to break the cycle that has defined your life up until now. It's about graduating from being a victim. Ask God to help you to do this. Break the cycle in your life and your family.

TAKE THE FIRST STEP—TAKE RESPONSIBILITY

Taking responsibility is the hardest thing for a man to do. Of all the "male issues," running away from responsibility is the foremost problem we face. Yet to become the man we want to become, the husband our wife needs us to be, and the father our children deserve means we must take responsibility for ourselves and our family.

LIVE FOR YOURSELF OR DIE FOR YOUR FAMILY

Having children is the ultimate rite of passage for a man. When kids come along, they need to be fed. They demand to be fed. They demand to be changed. Faced with that, a man usually goes one of two ways.

A man may decide it's all too much. He starts to withdraw... from his wife and from his children.

Or his character really kicks in. He begins to live for his family. He begins to live for someone other than himself.

It's all about character. Everything we are ever faced with, everything we ever deal with, everything we go through—the issue is always character.

MADE A MISTAKE, OWN IT

In my family, taking personal responsibility is part of the family fabric. I suppose I inherited it from my parents. Dad was 18 when he got married. Mom was pregnant. Both sets of grandparents were saying, "Have an abortion; this child is a mistake." Mom and Dad made the decision and said, "No."

So my Dad started as an electrical apprentice at a steel mill. After a while he realized he wanted more from his career and he started studying for a degree in engineering. But with a family to feed and a full-time job, degrees don't come easy.

It took my dad 16 years to earn that degree—16 years of dedicated part-time study. His strength of purpose was phenomenal.

My mom had two kids. She made a home, balanced a budget down to the pennies, and would walk miles to get the best deal on food stamps. She shunned her legal career and became a teacher so she could be home when we were home from school.

Selfless living. They faced the consequences of their actions. They had me. They raised me.

I know this goes against the grain of our thinking and philosophy, but my opinion is that abortion has become an excuse of an opulent, self-indulgent, self-absorbed Western world where people view their sin as something they can escape from instead of something they need to be cleansed from and take responsibility for.

Abortion causes grief of such an unimaginable degree, to both men and women—a grief far greater than choosing adoption. I deal with men and women all the time who are haunted, emotionally and physically, by the memories, people who outside of this have no hope of ever being freed from the error of their ways.

Through it all my parents did their best by their family. I saw my dad turn down some promotions because of the effect it would have on us. I grew up with my parents living for the greater responsibility. Sure, there were a lot of things along the way that today he wishes he'd done differently, but personal responsibility was a constant theme, and it's been passed on to me. It's part of my fabric now.

So I respect my dad for taking responsibility for the mistake he made in his late teens—a mistake that was going to affect him for the rest of his life. He could have run away, but he didn't. He owned it. That's what he modeled to me, his son—that kind of ownership, that kind of not talking to you as a friend but as a father.

This is something you should and must build into the fabric of your children. When you take responsibility, you take the first steps toward manhood.

Victims No More

How can someone who has come from a background of evading or running away from responsibility achieve a turnaround? It's all about breaking away from the idea that "I am a victim."

There's a strong thread of "victim culture" or "victim mentality" in our society. I believe it's a by-product of the welfare state introduced more than two full generations ago. Under the welfare state, somebody else will pay for the mistakes you make: "If I get my girlfriend pregnant, the state will look after her."

"If I lose my job, the government will pay me."

It's very tempting to let someone else take the fall. To be a dad, though, there has to come a point when we stop blaming other people for our past and start taking responsibility for our future. We have to say, "This is my life, my wife, my kids." That's the point at which you start to have a real life. That's the time you graduate from boy to man.

As mentioned before, maturity is not an issue of age; it starts with the acceptance of responsibility. Fathers, like mothers, are not born. Men grow into fathers—and fathering is a very important stage in their development.

Your Past Will Confine or Refine You

It's a principle that's worth repeating, or even putting on your wall: *Your past will either confine you or refine you.*

If you refuse to accept responsibility for your life, your past will put you in a cage. If you take responsibility for it, though, that same past will help you and refine you and make you into who you are supposed to be.

So many people are choosing to be confined by their past rather than be refined by it. It's like the old saying about the guy without any shoes—he used to complain until he met a man without feet.

I have heard so many stories and met so many people from worse backgrounds than mine who have risen to become phenomenally fruitful and successful in every area of their lives. I've noticed this about them: they have a sweetness of spirit that comes from the fact that they really value their lives. That's what I mean by our past refining us. When we accept where we have come from, we truly value where we are today. And we can see the awesome possibilities ahead of us.

THE "STUFF" OF LIFE

Everybody has "stuff." We're all on a journey toward a better life as a better person. We're all in a process. What we're fundamentally processing is our stuff: our baggage, problems, insecurities, battles, history, shadows, doubts, and fears.

One of my great friends is a Maori lady we will call "Lisa." She is one of my heroes. Her personal history is one of the most horrendous stories I have ever heard. Sexually abused by her uncle, she ran away from home at 17 to get married, only to end up in a situation far worse. Three marriages later, all she had ever known was violence, rape, and torment.

Today, you would just have no idea that her past was so awful. If you met her in the street, you would probably think she was one of those "lucky ones" who had never had a bad day. However, that was not how it was when I first met Lisa. She could have stayed mired in blame and unforgiveness for the rest of her life.

For three years my wife and I walked with her as she took responsibility for her own life. Her acceptance of and ability to own her own "stuff" were awe-inspiring.

I saw Lisa's attitude change. I saw her sweetness of spirit rise and take hold of her future as she came to terms with the issues in her past. One of my life's greatest moments was when I gave her away at her wedding to a wonderful man.

RELAX AND GET BETTER

We all have "stuff." We're dealing with it. I think we get a little uptight and cerebral about that fact. Everybody's going through it, so we should just relax a little and settle into a life journey—not a struggle, but a discovery.

We're not trying to be perfect dads. We're trying to deal with our stuff . We're loving our kids. We're making mistakes. We're getting better at it.

Nearly every day some issue comes up and I ask Beccy, "Did I do the right thing? How have I done?" I'm always consciously checking myself to see if I handled the kids right. I need to do that, because I mess it up all the time. I'm relaxed about that, though, because I know I'm committed to progressing, changing, and challenging, for my kids. For my wife I want to be a better husband every day. I want to be a better father every day. So I simply take responsibility for asking myself those questions and learning from my mistakes.

FATHERS, LIKE MOTHERS, ARE
NOT BORN. MEN GROW INTO
FATHERS—AND FATHERING
IS A VERY IMPORTANT STAGE
IN THEIR DEVELOPMENT.

David M. Gottesman

Saying Sorry, Asking for Forgiveness

Get into an early habit of saying sorry to your wife and your children. I started saying sorry to Jessica when she was just 12 months old. I had reacted poorly to something she had done. So even though she didn't understand what I was doing, I sat her down, crouched down in front of her, and apologized to her. My aim was to get into the habit of apologizing to her early on. We form the fabric of our families by creating habits like these.

I think apologies are very important. Saying sorry doesn't come easily to everyone; how much harder when the one you're apologizing to is "just a kid."

That first apology was the foundation of the environment we now have in our family. I'll say sorry to Jessica or Noah and they'll say, "Well, that's okay, Daddy." They understand the process: out of apology comes forgiveness, and from forgiveness grows reconciliation.

It started with me, but now it works both ways. My children know that they, too, can apologize if they have done something inappropriate. Dad, in turn, will say, "Well, that's okay. I forgive you."

So instead of just sweeping things under the carpet and hoping they go away, the children have learned how to repent, how to ask forgiveness, how to receive forgiveness, and how to forgive. I am modeling something far more important. I am modeling repentance, redemption, and restoration.

Too Proud to Say You're Sorry?

The idea that it's weak to ask for forgiveness is rooted in pride. If you've reacted rather than responded to a situation, are you too proud to ask your 3 or 4-year-old child to forgive you? You've raised your voice when you shouldn't have. Should you say nothing? If you don't model a repentant heart, who else will your children learn it from? You are sowing the seeds that will become ugly fruit in the life of your teenager.

There have been times when Beccy had asked the children not to do something, then I came along and unwittingly said the opposite: "You *can* do that." I crossed over Beccy's line of authority. I had to stop and apologize, both to Beccy, for undermining her, and to the children, for undermining their mother. Publicly.

"Jessie, Noah. Dad just wants to say sorry to Mom, because Dad didn't know Mom asked you not to do that. Mom asked you to do something and I'm going to support Mom in what she's asked you to do. Dad was wrong." Very clear. Very precise. Unambiguous.

There's nothing weak about communicating how strong and clear your commitment to your wife is. It's not weak to show that as parents you can't (and won't) be played off against each other. This house will not be divided. We will stand on our decisions. I will support their mother.

That's not a weak position; it's a strong one. If I violate it by undermining Beccy, it would be weak *not* to apologize. And Beccy takes exactly the same stance and supports me in the same manner.

Because my children have seen Beccy and I apologize to each other and to them, our children ask for forgiveness very easily. We readily give it.

The Power of Saying Sorry

We all know the power of saying sorry. I know a family that had a very damaging approach to family arguments. They'd yell and scream in the living room, then storm off and slam the bedroom doors.

It could be anything from four hours to a whole day before the doors were opened again. Life would go on as if the argument never happened. The whole event was ignored. It didn't matter who was bitter or hurt, there'd be no discussion.

As a result, all three children grew up with resentment toward their father. All three took major attitudes with them into adult life, with seemingly insurmountable bitterness toward their family.

One child, though, decided that enough was enough. Believing in the value of apologizing, she apologized for her own part in the family bitterness. That child was actually the seed that changed the entire family.

CREATE A CULTURE

If only that dad had created a culture of apology and forgiveness in his family during their childhood, years of wasted bitterness could have been redeemed.

A culture doesn't just happen. You create a culture. That's why I began apologizing to my children before they had any notion of what I was doing. That's why I started kissing them, hugging them, and telling them I love them, early and often. To create a culture, behavior has to be habitual. Better for me to learn how to apologize early on rather than struggle with it later.

A culture doesn't just happen. You create a culture.

When she was just 4 years old, Jessica came to me and said, "Daddy, I need to ask you to forgive me, 'coz I did sumthing."

This showed me that the channels of communication in my family had been clearly defined. My children know that forgiveness follows repentance. So when something happens, they come to me to acknowledge what they have done instead of running from it.

I'm certain that if I did not make a standard policy of apologizing for my errors, then my children would find it hard to apologize for their own mistakes. When Jessica came solemnly to me, I responded solemnly. I didn't make light of it. I sat down and looked her in the eyes. We talked and prayed.

The way someone repents to you is the spirit in which you should respond. If they are nonchalant, it means nothing. But if it is heartfelt, look them in the eyes and accept with humility their repentant words.

Consequences Without Condemnation

Please don't get me wrong here. I'm not saying that a child who shotguns apologies should be let off scot-free. I'm not saying that a child can escape all consequences simply by saying sorry. They must understand that there are ramifications.

What we do in our home is say, "Yes, we accept your apology, but your actions have consequences. You have done this and although you are forgiven, here is the consequence of your action. Here's the punishment."

The forgiveness is unconditional, but children must understand that they reap what they sow. A family culture that embraces apology and forgiveness can eliminate the seeds of bitterness, resentment, and rebellion before they have a chance to grow.

Breaking the Cycle

Isn't it horrible when you see your children repeating the mistakes you've made? Reproducing after your own kind, you might say. Have you ever caught yourself disciplining your children for the faults you find in yourself? I hate that, yet it is so human to repeat patterns from one generation to the next.

Sometimes the repetition is positive. Yet so often it is not.

If your dad is loving...you probably will be.

If your dad is an alcoholic...you probably will be.

If your dad loves your mom...you will probably love your wife.

If your dad hurts your mom...you will probably repeat that.

Take heart. Even the worst of us can be transformed. We can break the cycle so our children don't become "undesirable" repetitions of ourselves but really positive expressions of the best aspects of our family heritage.

FROM CURSE TO COVENANT—START A NEW GENERATION

When I became a dad, I realized I had some issues in this area. I'd received a model of fatherhood from my own father; but as I've said, he didn't really know how to be a dad. The reason he didn't know was because his dad hadn't known...and so on back through the generations. I could see for myself that I was at least the third generation of men who didn't know how to be a father or, rather, had inappropriate models to follow.

Something was getting in the way of good fathering in my family. I knew I had to break that something. You could call it a cycle—I call it a curse. I was determined to break the curse and replace it with something far better: a covenant between God, my family, and me. A covenant is a solemn agreement that is binding on all parties. The covenant I made was to be a good husband and a good father. That was the decision I made, believing the curse of the previous generations to be broken.

It was like breaking down an old tarnished wall around my soul and rebuilding a new one. I went looking for material to help me fulfill my covenant with my family: good books, good friends, and good courses on being a husband and father—the more *practical*, the better.

If you see patterns in your family line that you don't want to pass on to the next generation, it's time to make your own new covenant with your family.

In the Bible God is pretty clear about the principle of inherited curses and blessings:

> *…He punishes the children and their children for the sin of the fathers to the third and fourth generation* (Exodus 34:7).

I've seen that principle at work in my own family and I'm sure you can in yours. A grandparent tells you about something that happened in their day and you think, "Wow, I've gone through the same thing." It's very disturbing when you see sin that happened a century ago still repeating itself in your family today.

The great news is there's a very positive side to the equation, which vividly shows God's generosity and love:

> *Know therefore that the Lord your God is God; He is the faithful God, keeping His covenant of love to a thousand generations of those who love Him and keep His commands* (Deuteronomy 7:9).

The picture is clear. If one generation sins, it passes that sin down the line. All the time I see men break the "covenant of love" they should have with their wives by committing adultery and inflicting verbal and mental abuse.

This kind of covenant-breaking sin may have robbed your family line of 75 to 100 years (for the last three to four generations).

One man's decision to get right with God takes effect immediately, and it touches a family forever. It breaks the cycle of the broken-hearted for up to 1,000 generations, or 25,000 years.

I don't know what you have had to face or to fear. But I do know that you don't have to tie yourself to the sins of the past. You can break the cycle and start a new generation today.

COLLECTIVE WISDOM

You need a license to drive a car, so you go to driving school. We serve our apprenticeship before we can build a house. Yet when we become parents there is no such thing as parents' school! In fact, the only teaching we receive in parenting is how we were parented ourselves. As you've just read, if your upbringing wasn't conducive to a balanced lifestyle or the development of a rounded person, then you will actually reproduce something in your children that isn't positive. It may even be destructive.

If you've come from that type of environment, you have to be honest about identifying it. You have to admit to yourself, "Yes, my parenting skills are not up to the challenge," and then ask, "What do I have to actively do to improve myself?"

Having a child is a commitment. Everybody gives lip service to that idea. As fathers, though, we have to be prepared to live it, not just say it. We're bringing a life into the world. We need to look at ourselves, search ourselves, and change ourselves in order to become a better parent—a better person, a better husband, a better father.

If we really see fatherhood as a commitment from day one, then we're prepared to develop skills in ourselves. This will hopefully start even before we have children.

When it comes to being a father, whatever you do, don't drive blind. Collective wisdom is the big thing. Observe other people's lives. Ask questions. Read books. Watch others. Attend seminars. Spend time reading websites about parenting and fatherhood. Talk to other dads. Ask them why they do what they do. Go after collective wisdom. Don't accept everything, but sift it until you find what fits you, your personality and your value system.

Life is like a smorgasbord. It's never an à la carte restaurant offering everything you need to know about marriage or fathering on one handy menu. No, there is a feast of choices and possibilities. You walk up to the table and literally eat from other people's lives. That's collective wisdom.

For instance, in our parenting experience, we know people who are very good with children when they're young. Other people we know are great with older kids. There are people who are very good with their marriage but hopeless with their kids. There are husbands who are very good with their wives, and wives who are very good with their husbands. So we have literally taken from a mixture of different people. Those are your driving lessons on the way to your license to drive a family.

When it comes to being a father, whatever you do, don't drive blind.

I know there is a strong perception within our culture that men are not as good as women at the relational. The perception is that women are far better at gathering wisdom on life from the people around them.

But if you think about it, it is actually quite natural for men to sit with other men and enrich one another. The issue really is that in modern society there's not a lot of space/time to just sit and kick around the general business of life.

Modern guys don't tend to get much further than talking about sports down at the pub—not the best environment for sharing collective wisdom.

But the major blockage is that we have to get past the idea that asking questions is an admission of failure or shortcoming. You know that feeling. It's a competitive thing. There are people in our lives who are able to help us answer the simple yet important questions we face daily:

"How do you balance the books?"

"How do you raise a family?"

"How do you prosper your family?"

"How do you love your wife?"

"How do you stay in love with her?"

"How do you address issues?"

"How do I travel and not destroy all I love?"

Be bold enough to ask the questions. Don't aim all your questions at one person. Find a range of people to ask.

Should dads get together? Coffee club for guys? It certainly works for women getting together for an hour on Saturday mornings to talk. I can't see why it can't work for guys.

I meet with a couple of close friends myself, actually. We get down under the surface to talk about deeper issues. But that's something I don't do naturally. Most guys don't. I do it *deliberately* because it's worthwhile. Besides that, I take the time to ask deliberate questions of people I admire. You'll find they are often flattered when you ask their opinion.

Recently a friend of mine went through a disastrous period with his 25-year-old daughter, so I asked him straight up, "Why did it happen? What did you miss? How would you do it differently?" His response: 60 minutes of brilliant and important information that will be stored away in my memory for future reference.

Even if you have no one to talk with, you can go after collective wisdom through books or the internet. You don't have to be isolated. In fact, being isolated is a choice. If you're scared after suddenly discovering "I'm a dad!" and you're freaking out and have no one to talk to, there are a range of organizations, products, and resources you can turn to for help.

Fatherhood isn't like riding the bus. The family won't steer itself for you. As a dad you're at the wheel: You set the pace; you determine the direction. Just know that there's no need to drive blind.

You can go into parenting with your eyes open, your skills up and a full license to drive your family. Get your license before you get your family!

PARENTHOOD REMAINS

THE GREATEST SINGLE

PRESERVE OF THE AMATEUR.

Alvin Toffler

Flight Check

When a pilot first settles into the plane's cockpit, he completes a flight check. When we're at the controls of our family, shouldn't we do the same? In terms of how we live our lives, men have a tendency to avoid self-checking. But there are three gauges I believe we should always keep an eye on: our *family* gauge, *social* gauge, and *business* gauge.

Also we need to be constantly aware of how these three gauges are registering, on three different levels: *spiritual*, *emotional*, and *physical*.

A flight check of your family life is particularly important, because the way we men are wired, our work life tends to get priority. If you're not checking your family life and making sure it maintains a balance, your family gauge is definitely going to go down.

Here's a thought for you: "Only the paranoid survive." That's the business mantra of Intel's co-founder, Andy Grove. It applies to a man's relationships, too. Relate it to your marriage: "Am I doing the right or wrong thing here?" "How am I going?" "Do I have the balance right; how am I weighing?" "Have I made time for the family this week?" "Is the gauge empty or is it full?"

It's the whole self-evaluation thing. I'm not suggesting that we have to become "navel gazers," but from everything I know about men, we need to deliberately make time for fleeting thoughts: a regular quick assessment of who we are and what we are about.

Getting the Trim Right—Feeling Fulfilled

A man has to balance his life. We get value from our work, whereas many women get their sense of value from a mix of their work, their relationships, and their family. Men love to work. We get immense satisfaction from it.

So when it comes to the flight check, you have to watch out for two warning signs:

1. Are you overcompensating and neglecting your immediate needs?

   If you're concentrating on your family and social life but your business life is on a downhill track, you're not going to feel fulfilled. Men need to work. Don't overcompensate by focusing entirely on the family and neglecting the work you love. It's about balance.

2. Are you stalling on the family and neglecting your long-term needs?

   Your work may give you immediate satisfaction, but a man has a long-term need to engage with his family. That is why you need to be continually checking the family gauge. If you are not fulfilled when it comes to your family, then your enjoyment of your work will only sustain you for a while. Eventually you'll fall victim to a great sense of dissatisfaction in your life. Again, it's about balance—but this is the factor that really needs your attention.

If you find you're low on your family gauge, don't knock yourself around with a false sense of guilt because you didn't give your family any time this week. Just correct the trim: Make sure you have time with the family next week. You've been away all week? No problem. When it comes to work, you have to do what you have to do. Next week *make* some time.

Redefine Yourself Daily

To be honest, by nature I'm a bit of a loner. The flight check strategy is essential for me. Checking my gauges keeps me aware of the cycles in my life—my emotional life. I'm aware of those things. I know what gives me highs. I know what brings on the lows. Keeping balanced isn't just for my own well-being; it's for my entire family.

I work in a people business, so I need to be constantly aware of my emotional gauge, because spending time with people is the most draining thing for me. I just couldn't do my work if I didn't make an active effort to evaluate what's good for me and what's not. I set up the things that work for me and try to avoid the thought processes and time wasters that lead me into my "black hole."

Once you get into the habit of self-evaluation, you'll be amazed how much choice and control you have over your own life.

An important truth to remember is that hardly anybody has it together totally. I certainly don't have it all together. But I try to redefine myself daily. There have been situations where I've blown it completely with my wife and my children. I don't get discouraged, though, because I know that my family is not like a house of cards that can't be rebuilt. We have a stronger foundation than that because I've made a habit of taking responsibility for myself. I complete the flight check, correct the trim, and we get back on course.

BEING THERE

I noticed that our daughter, Jessica, went through a very Daddy-dependant stage at around 4 years of age. She really wanted Daddy to be there. She needed a sense of security from me. A year or so later, that came to an end. She moved from Daddy-dependence to being the most secure child in her group of friends. She wasn't the most outgoing or the most boisterous, but she was certainly the most secure in her group of friends, many of whom don't have dads who are actively involved.

They say a child gets its character from its mother and its security from its father. I have found that to be very true. There's one main way in which a dad provides a sense of security: by being there.

Try to be the first and last thing they see each day. If you're home late and your children are asleep, scoop them up, and kiss them awake. Then nestle them back to sleep. They will sleep more soundly because Daddy is home and their world is more secure.

Dad, you have to be there. Parenting is not a single-parent activity. You ask any single mom or any single dad and they'll tell you that single parenting is not how it's supposed to be.

I've seen it myself, even when I've been away on business for just a short while. My wife experiences a strong sense of relief when I'm home and I'm involved with the kids again. It's amazing how much *stress* comes on the family when I'm away for only three weeks.

So what do you do when you're in the middle of busy things? Do something consistently! Small but consistent interaction creates a pattern of involvement that will give your children the sense of security they desperately need.

I find that my *consistent* presence at breakfast makes a lot of difference. If you're heading out of town, get the kids up early for breakfast. If they're young, they'll be having a sleep in the afternoon anyway, so get them up half an hour earlier to have coffee and toast with Dad (and make breakfast for Mom in bed as a special "together" activity!).

Dad, you have to be there. Parenting is not a single-parent activity.

Take your daughter and son on "Daddy dates" to the local café or movie theatre. I regularly take my children on Daddy dates. For one thing, it gives Mom a break. It also gives them focused time with Dad. They need that. At the same time—and we'll get into this in more detail later—it models adult relationships. Your kids will learn *how to treat people* and *how to be treated* from the time you spend with them.

An Everyday Commitment

Kids are an *everyday* commitment, not a holiday package you schedule for two weeks a year for them. Dad for 30 minutes a day, every day, is better than 24/7 for two weeks on the family vacation.

I have been known to travel a round trip of 90 minutes from the office just to grab 30 minutes at home with the family before heading back to work! In one week I did that several times, just to get in some consistent encounters with my kids.

That extra mileage in the car is a price, but Dad's career does come at a price. The question is: who's going to pay the price? I think *I* should. I'm the one who was away. It should be me who pays the price. If coming home and spending an hour with my children means I have to stay up for an hour working, I'll do it. If spending time with my kids means I have to work in the evening instead of watching the program I want to see on TV, then I'll just have to tape it and try to catch it later. I'm absolutely determined that my wife and children will not pay the price that allows me to do the work I love to do. I want to conquer the world, but my family is not a price I am prepared to pay.

FATHER TIME

As fathers, one of the areas we must take responsibility for is time. If I mismanage my schedule, someone has to take responsibility for my actions.

Will it be my family or will it be me?

Do my kids need me? Done. I'll come home to spend some time with them, then go back to the office. I might not get home again until 9 P.M., but I've had some significant time with my children...and it's been *me* who has paid the price.

Face it, dads, there's not a lot of room for dead time in a father's life. This is a time-deficient world in which we live. Make use of your time wisely.

Being there for your family is not just good for your wife and children; it's good for you, too! When it comes to developing your character and your life, your wife and children are the most important influencers you will ever have.

Remember, you only have your children for a short two dozen or so years. Don't waste the time you have with them!

On-the-Road Rules

Road Warriors Can Win

Bill Hendricks and Jim Coté worked for a battery business in the United States. At a company picnic they casually asked some of the workers' wives what they thought about their husbands being out on the road so often. Jim discovered why his company had one of the highest divorce rates in America. The company had placed a heavy burden on families by sending their "road warriors" away from home on business so much.

Few of my peers are out on the road as much as I. In the course of my ministry and business work, my family and I spend six months of each year in the United States and six months in the Pacific region. We are in a constant state of going somewhere. Beccy and I made the decision to take our kids on the road and home-school them ourselves. We think it's more important for our children to be part of our family system than part of the school system. They won't miss out on life experiences. Rather, our time on the road has given them an abundance of enriching inputs as well as high scholastic achievement.

But sometimes you just can't be there. If you add it up at the end of the year, you could be away for an average of three or four days a week. You have to do it, though, because you're on commission, or it's your portfolio or your company, and if you're not away, you're not making money.

So what do you do? Here are some rules for life on the road that I've found very useful.

Out of Sight But Not Out of Mind

Every night I interact with my wife and kids. I call them, e-mail them, and pray with them over the phone. Or even if I can't get in touch, I'll still sit down and pray for them, hold a picture, look at them. To me, that "touchy feely" stuff is a matter of family survival.

Out on the road, with my head full of all the other things around me, my mind can start heading in some destructive directions. But if my wife fills my mind and my children fill my dreams, I am less likely to make the destructive mistakes others have made.

Always in Touch

Since my children have been old enough to dial a phone, they know how to get hold of Dad if they want to talk. It doesn't matter what meeting I'm in or who I'm with. I've sat across from major clients as the phone silently vibrated with "home" on the screen. I've looked into a CEO's eyes and said, "Excuse me, my family's calling." I've sat there, fully aware that this man is listening to me listening to a story about Barbie's new dress. I've stared down the silent rebukes that are brought about more by the CEO's guilt at his own destroyed family than the interruption to our meeting. However, in most cases it has opened up a great conversation about how to balance life and love.

My kids don't abuse this, though. They know that if I say, "I have to go, but I'll call you back," then they'll be hearing from me soon. But they always know Daddy will take their call, because Daddy keeps his word.

At Home the Kids Are the Focus

I try to give my children slabs of time and not get distracted. If I get home at 6 P.M. and they go to bed at 8 P.M., I know I have two hours to give them. If I can't because I have to prepare for the next day, I'll give them as much undivided attention as I can. No phone calls, no newspapers. Lots of eye contact and lots of cuddles—whether they are 6 or 16. A teenager still needs and wants it. This stuff is glue that holds a family together through the challenging times.

TAKE THE FAMILY ON THE ROAD

Yes, I take my family on business trips. I make my family part of my lifestyle. Remember, I married my best friend, not my company. My first job involving major car travel clocked up more than 40,000 miles a year. So I took the family! It didn't cost the company a dollar extra and our young family had some great times traveling together. While Daddy went to appointments to make money, the girls went to the shops to spend it—a win/win situation!

With my last two employers, I made it a point to negotiate family time into my contract. The rule of thumb: For every week away, my family gets a solid 24 hours on my return. So if I'm away for three weeks, my first three days back are spent at home.

If my family pays a price to grow the company, the company can pay the price of letting me reconnect.

HURRY HOME

Life on the road can be seductive...nice hotel, no screaming kids, no house chores, just the comfortable drone of Fox News and room service. My rule is: hurry home.

If I'm away for five days, I'll make sure I travel all night so I can be home first thing for breakfast on the sixth day. That way I can have the full day with my family. It costs me personally in travel time, but the family doesn't go an extra day without Dad. It minimizes the impact of your travel on your family.

FAMILY PLANNING

My family feels like they are part of what I do because we have open discussions about where I'm going and what I'll be doing. "Dad's away for business." "Dad's having a meeting; this is part of what Dad's doing." "Dad's helping some men."

We have a map so they can see where Dad is going. We have a family calendar so the kids can count down the days until I come home. All of these little things make up a part of the whole.

AWAY, BUT ACTIVELY ENGAGED

Spend 10 minutes talking with your child on the phone. Yeah, it costs you two or three dollars, but it's worth it so they know they have your undivided attention as they tell you about all the important things in their life.

Buy a digital camera for your laptop. Every day I talk to the kids in real time with video conferencing. It has made a huge difference in how I (and they) cope with the stress of life on the road.

Hey, these rules apply *even if you don't travel!* Many dads may be at home, but they're so detached that they may as well be on the road. They're not focused, they're not imparting, and they're not impacting their family life. They're not joined with their family.

Being an absent father isn't about being divorced. It's about being detached. Plug in!

MY FATHER USED TO SAY,

LET THEM SEE YOU AND NOT

THE SUIT. THAT SHOULD

BE SECONDARY.

Cary Grant

Sometimes Someone Else Needs To Be There

We have our children for only a very short time, so we must try our best to give them everything they need for the rest of their lives. One thing our children really need is a source of insight and advice to help them chart a course through life.

As their father you should be the strongest voice. But there should be other streams, too. Other adults should be making an investment of care in your children's lives. These key nonparent relationships are very important. As a dad I'm not always going to be able to hear what my children are saying, try as I might. They need to have other people to go to: Uncle Andrew's house or Cousin Jack's place, for instance.

These trusted family friends will echo what you would have said anyway—not by design or pre-planning, but simply because the relationships you have with these trustworthy men are based on shared values and beliefs. These guys can reinforce your own family values. Sometimes it's easier for a child to hear words of wisdom from someone who isn't their parent.

Consider this as building safety fences along the cliffs of your children's lives, so when they come to a major conflict and they just can't hear Dad or Mom's voice, there are other people they can go to, to affirm the values that should be driving their lives.

If you leave it up to your children to choose which "streams of wisdom" they go to in a time of crisis, they'll probably choose their friends. But you and I know that friends can't offer the kind of moral support or insightful wisdom that takes a lifetime to develop. That's an adult's job. That's why it's important to build a community of caring adults around your children—a community with eyes to the future, a network of friends and supporters.

The people we allow our children to spend the most time with have similar moral values to us, of course, but they also have similar expectations about how kids should behave. They're people who will reinforce the things we hold dearest.

Of course this network isn't just for crisis times, but for general fun and family times, too. The community you build around your children will create memories and stay with them for the rest of their lives.

Dads and Careers

It's the one weekend you had set aside for your family. It's all planned: games, a walk, seeing a movie together. Good, simple family stuff. Then you get "the call." An important client is flying in from overseas; there will be a business meeting, followed by golf. Sorry, kids.

Why is it so important to meet that client? Why is it permissible to disappoint your kids? Why? Your family has been robbed by your work.

The revelation we need to have as dads is this: *It's just as important to further your family as it is to further your career.* You must give yourself freedom to make it a priority to take your child to the library or to the college function, or to be a disc jockey at their preschool's disco.

WE HAVE TO REDEFINE SUCCESS

We see prosperity as how much money we can put in the bank. Shouldn't it rather be the whole quality of our lifestyle?

There's the familiar saying: "No one ever died saying, 'I wish I'd spent more time at the office.'" The deathbed confession of a career-driven man is all too often: "I wish I'd spent more time with my family, my children."

True wealth is wealth of experience, wealth of life!

The pot of gold at the end of the rainbow is nothing but fool's gold. As men we've been raised and cultured to believe that material wealth is the most significant and important thing in life. Instead, that path just leads to the all-too-common scenario of a wealthy man dying alone in a grandiose house with not a lot of love around him. That's not wealth. It's not worth sacrificing your wife and family for something like that. True wealth is wealth of experience, wealth of life!

I'm not saying, "Turn your back on material success." No way. It's a very big part of a man's life. Men naturally define themselves by what they do. But *family* has to be rated first among our successes and achievements. If we were to rate our success in *family* like we score our golf game or racquetball, how would we score?

True wealth is wealth of experience, wealth of life!

Generation Xcellence

A quiet revolution has been taking place. The '80s were all about the Gordon Gekko-style "greed is good" maxim of the baby boomers. Since then, a whole new generation has started coming through—Generation X—and they want something different from life.

Family is very important to Generation Xers. As kids they saw the demands of corporate structure destroy their families. They do not want that to happen to them.

Yet corporate structure hasn't really changed to meet this need. There's a bit of lip service to the needs of family, but *it takes determination to put limits on your company's voracious appetite for your life.* I'd like to say that in the modern world, any corporation that is too greedy when it comes to its employees' lives is dooming itself. Sadly, I don't think that's true…just yet. Why? Not enough people have said "Enough!"

But I do think it's possible to keep your job and fence off time for your family. I believe that this generation is getting close to forcing a transformation. Either people will become self-employed, or corporations will change and accept that there are boundaries around people's lives.

If you see people as valuable, then you realize that corporations are *privileged* to be able to employ people. Do you see it that way? Are your employers privileged to have you on their team? They sure are! Do you, as an employer, see the value of your staff?

The move toward this enlightened state has largely been driven by the women's movement. They've been saying, "We want to have kids *and* we want to go to work." Well, now men are starting to say similar things:

"Yes, I want to work, but I want to be a father to my kids."

"Yes, it's valid for me to take paternity leave: a day here and there to take my son or daughter fishing."

"Yes, this is what makes me a *whole person*. I'm not just an army of one!" Some organizations are waking up to the fact that *a person whose private life is in balance functions much better as a productive employee.* Yet we continue to emphasize public performance at private expense.

For generations companies have been saying, "Our people are our greatest asset." It's time for them to start walking the talk. Believe me, companies won't change unless we make them.

Daniel Petrie, former head of Microsoft Australia, came to the conclusion that the corporate world does not cater to fathers. In his book, *Father Time*, Daniel wrote:

> Through the last 50 or so years we (men) have created business infrastructures that are basically anti-children, anti-family, anti-spouse, anti-community and anti-anything approaching social responsibility. These infrastructures are pro-profit. This is seen as the ultimate excuse.[1]

He's saying that men built those structures. Men are going to have to rebuild them, in a new shape that gives us room to be fathers.

So why isn't it happening more rapidly?

Because the companies themselves aren't motivated to change. Baby boomers are still in control, and X-generation fathers are not being forceful enough to put pressure on them to change.

Daniel Petrie doesn't lay all the blame at the companies' feet. He points out that in the corporate arena, men just haven't been strong in asserting their rights as fathers.

You can have a family and a career. You're just going to have to assert yourself.

Fortunately, it's in our nature as men to do just that! There is nothing like a good challenge to bring greatness out in a man.

ENDNOTE

1. Daniel Petrie, *Father Time*, (Jane Curry Publishing, 2005).

THE FAMILY IS THE CORNERSTONE OF OUR SOCIETY. MORE THAN ANY OTHER FORCE, IT SHAPES THE ATTITUDE, THE HOPES, THE AMBITIONS, AND THE VALUES OF THE CHILD. AND WHEN THE FAMILY COLLAPSES, IT IS THE CHILDREN THAT ARE USUALLY DAMAGED. WHEN IT HAPPENS ON A MASSIVE SCALE, THE COMMUNITY ITSELF IS CRIPPLED. SO UNLESS WE WORK TO STRENGTHEN THE FAMILY, TO CREATE CONDITIONS UNDER WHICH MOST PARENTS WILL STAY TOGETHER, ALL THE REST—— SCHOOLS, PLAYGROUNDS, PUBLIC ASSISTANCE, AND PRIVATE CONCERN WILL NEVER BE ENOUGH.

Lyndon Baines Johnson

Permission to Break the Chains

The first dozen years of my career were spent in a large corporate organization. It was a dynamic, exciting place to be, but like most corporations, it demanded a lot from its people.

I mean *a lot*.

Everything was sacrificed to the needs of my employer, including my family and my relationships.

I was just starting out with the company; I had yet to earn my stripes. Because of my broken background as a child, I was so desperate for affirmation that I would not assert myself or the desperate needs I felt for my family. Hear me now: I was the problem. This was my issue.

I didn't have a sense of having "permission" to love my family. Like so many men in business, I couldn't say to myself, without guilt:

- ❖ "I am allowed to say 'no' to work demands."
- ❖ "I am allowed to set my own agenda for how I run my family."
- ❖ "I am allowed to love my wife and give her the time she needs."
- ❖ "I am allowed to love my kids and put their occasional demands first."

It took me many years to get permission to do those things. The permission didn't come from supervisors, team leaders, managers, or bosses. Permission to love my family, to lead my family, to put my family on top of my priority list, had to come from *me*.

And in order to do that, I decided to downscale my life.

It Was All Greek to Me

This permission-giving is a decision that men tend to make in their 30s when they ask: "Am I going to give myself permission to take control of my life rather than leave control in the hands of other people?"

It's about the difference between the Greek and Hebrew approaches to excellence. I'd been living the Greek way, but now I've chosen the Hebrew way and I'm loving it.

Unfortunately, most large organizations lose sight of the value of the individual as a *whole person*. They see an individual as a component that fulfills a position from 8 A.M. until 6 P.M. To function successfully, they can only really concern themselves with those 10 hours in a person's day. But behind each person is another 14 hours that make up the complete picture.

Because organizations don't see the whole picture, they expect you to give your all for the corporate vision. You're expected to die for the cause. You have to strive to be the best, the greatest, the biggest. That's the corporate world's version of individual excellence, and that, my friend, is a very *Greek* way of looking at the world.

How does the Hebrew view measure up? The Hebrew worldview has its starting point in the relationship between God and man, which then expanded into God and family. Only after that relationship was firmly established did God give man the instruction to have dominion over the world. The central focus remains the individual's relationships with God and family. So when a Hebrew-oriented individual does dynamic and active things in the world, they do so in the context of family.

The Greek model is about the individual excelling for the sake of the individual. Look around and you'll see that our culture is essentially based on a set of Greek-style philosophies. Today we call it "humanism," yet it is the most "unhuman" philosophy around! Individual success is what it's all about—in life, business, love, sports...you name it—as opposed to the Hebrew worldview, which is much more family-based, more collective.

Well, I decided to switch my perspective from Greek to Hebrew. I no longer based my personal well-being on Greek philosophy but on biblical theology. I gave myself permission to assert my full identity as John King—not just as a corporate man but as a God-and-family man, too.

Declaring Independence

How did it go down in the corporate world when I decided to give myself this permission to have some independence and family commitment? It was a case of running flat out on someone else's treadmill.

It was a constant battle! There was always another meeting to attend. At the end of the week there'd be no time left—no time to sit down and reflect, no meaningful time left for my family, no time to hang out with my kids or go to school activities. I was always tired, always busy, always preoccupied.

A case of running flat out on someone else's treadmill.

I loved where I worked. I loved the people. I loved the excitement, the rush of it all. But it simply was not possible for me to work in the corporate structure and live according to all my values. Sure, it was great to be part of something so massive and life changing, but eventually it all just turned out to be a case of running flat out on someone else's treadmill.

Beccy and I decided to check right out of the system. We stepped out on our own. It is very empowering to live like this. You have a sense of your own self-worth and identity. It has been great—what a fantastic place we are in as a family. It's worth the sacrifice and the change in relationships and friendships. It's worth the change to obtain that sense of control. It's worth it to know I'll be leaving behind a legacy in the form of my children's children that will outlast anything and anyone I worked for. To be sure of leaving that legacy, I had to give myself permission to break the chains of corporate structure. I did it. Maybe you'll have to do it too. Or maybe you can persuade your corporate organization to see you as a whole person and support your commitment to your kids.

I recently returned to my first place of employment, and the change I saw was startling: There was a corporate day-care center and a preschool. In the years after we left, they had changed the way they operated to keep their best people around. They came to realize that a healthy, happy family makes a healthy, happy staff, which makes a healthy, happy company!

Downsizing for a Bigger Soul

I'm always keen to talk to other people about their families. I've always seen it as a way to equip myself as a father and improve myself as a husband. While out shopping with Beccy one day, we met a lady who told us about her son and daughter-in-law. Both of them were professional people who had each been making upward of $100,000 a year.

They'd been married for more than a year when they literally looked at each other one day and said: "Why are we doing what we're doing? We got married because we loved each other. We got married because we wanted to have a family. But here we are, so pressured, each working 60 or so hours a week. We don't see each other any more. This is not the sort of family we want."

So they both quit. They downsized.

They had kids. She stayed home. He found a job earning half the money. They sold out of their uptown lifestyle and bought a house in a more suburban area. They did this because they realized they were not living in line with what they valued.

That really got me thinking. Most of us grew up seeing our parents go after the mighty dollar. That's what we learned, so most of us are doing the same thing now. It's a spiral and we're willingly caught in it. Some of us, though, have a moment of clarity when we think: "There has to be more to life than hungering after big bucks."

Well, guys, if you need permission to go after what's more important in life, I'm giving it to you. Scale your income down by 20 percent and your quality of life will increase by 60 percent.

I think you can do it. I think you *should* do it. Men like challenges. Well, here's a challenge for you: Step out of the high-pressured, high-paying style of life. Take a step down. Scale down your income and actually increase the quality of your life.

Your initial "step back" will actually turn around in a few short years. On average, in three years most guys find themselves overtaking their "old peers"… whose lives are shipwrecked: their marriages ending in divorce, their assets divided, and their lives destroyed. On the other hand, here you are, going from strength to strength, building a foundation that will last you a lifetime.

Many people are taking this step. Downsizing started with corporations, and then the people who were being downsized realized they could do the same thing, too. Masses of people began working from home because it meant they could spend more time with their families.

Why did they want to do this? Because as children they'd seen the corporate world running their family life…and ruining it. People just don't want to do that any more.

I actually think we now have a whole generation of people who are "checking out" of the corporate treadmill because they realize the importance of family. These people are a by-product of broken marriages and broken relationships. Now that Generation Xers are becoming parents, husbands, and wives, they're saying, "Hey, I don't want to be like Dad and Mom. I want to have time for my family. I want my family to *rub off on me!*"

What Are We Doing It For?

What do all those dollars do for you anyway? We use most of our money simply to enable us to do the things that satisfy us. If we decide to restrict the flow of dollars, does that mean we can never have fun again? No way. It just means we have to redefine the things that satisfy us.

People who aren't reliant on dollars find a lot of other ways to have fun. Growing up as kids, we didn't have a lot of money in our house, but some of my fondest memories are times away with my family. Camping, playing in backyards...even just playing with the water hose was hours of fun.

Don't kid yourself that your children really need you to have lots of disposable income. They don't really need both parents working, with a double income, a double mortgage, and a big house. Your children would rather have you, even if it's you on a lower budget.

Making your family a bigger part of your life is certainly going to make up for a smaller income. Downsizing is a great deal: You get to swap high income for low stress. You may have to live with smaller material aspirations for a season, but you'll enjoy much bigger helpings of love, satisfaction, and family.

I'm not talking about confining yourself to poverty. I'm talking about slowing down so you can run together.

Fathers Can Transform Families

I spent many years involved in youth work. It was hugely rewarding, but there was also the tragic aspect of being an eyewitness to the destruction of young lives. I remember a young girl we picked up off the street and brought back to our youth service. On that particular evening, I think 10 or 15 guys had been having their way with her. It wasn't gang rape, as such, so much as a consenting orgy.

We contacted her mother to come for her, and I'll never forget the way her mother sat with her in our office and called her daughter a "slut." I thought: *"Mom, your words have framed your daughter's world. Maybe you've called her a slut so many times, it's established the way she sees herself."*

It was astonishing to sit down with this girl and watch her relate with both her parents. The family was very affluent and very influential in the community. Dad was a pilot for a major airline. He was away a lot and not at all active in the family. He sat there in the midst of this turmoil, totally disinterested. He'd opted out of any sense of authority or leadership in the family.

A young lady gets a sense of uniqueness and value from her relationship with her dad. But that had been taken away from this girl. Her sense of emotional security just wasn't there. She was out there looking for strong male love, affirmation, and acceptance…but in all the wrong places.

Mom was obviously in anguish. She didn't know what to do. But you know, there's really no point in yelling at a kid for what she's done as a teenager when she's been allowed to go her own way her whole life. That child had become exactly what her parents had allowed her to become. If you allow a child to throw a tantrum at three years of age, they will still be doing it at 20. Remember you are Dad—the all-powerful, all-seeing, all-knowing creator of their world. You can make it heaven or hell—*it's your choice.*

The girl's whole peer group of rich local kids had the same outlook. Every holiday they would go from house to house, drinking all the alcohol in each place, then move on. Each kid would have upwards of $100 a week to spend on whatever they wanted. They'd spend the whole summer getting drunk, stoned, and having sex. Their average age was 13 years.

The first case of **AIDS** I ever had to confront came out of this group. It was inevitable, really. The girl got pregnant and the guy had HIV.

And the parents? Did they know about all this? Yes, because we informed them. They did nothing about it. They were comfortable with the group their kids were running with. Maybe they didn't think it was their concern? Maybe they felt they didn't have a right to get involved? That was their justification. Either way, they were wrong. Parents *must* get involved in this sort of destructive behavior—do what it takes to get their family back on track. Every one of these children lived in a million-dollar home paid for by parents working two jobs to pay the mortgage. One absentee parent is tragic enough—two absentee parents results in the destruction of children's lives.

It's Not Over
Until It's Over

Every child is looking for Dad. When Dad starts being Dad, you get into the whole prodigal son situation. The prodigal son, as Jesus told it, was a wayward guy who turned his back on his dad. After years of traveling and spending his inheritance, he headed back home looking for Dad. The son was shocked to the core when he came back expecting rejection but found that his father's love was indestructible. If you are prepared to be Dad, if you are prepared to change, there will come a time when your children will come back around. It's yet another example of the power of a dad: If Dad changes, the whole family will be transformed.

I knew a guy who had been a prominent crime figure in Sydney's Kings Cross area, the black heart of Australia's crime scene and sex industry. This guy had been a horrendous man to deal with in his younger days; his family turned out the same way because they'd been brought up in the whole atmosphere of the sex and drugs business.

His wife left him. His kids were totally alienated from him. They had no relationship with their dad. In fact, they hated their father for all he had done to them. This family had completely broken down.

Enter Jesus Christ. Enter the Man who specializes in raising things from the dead! Result: The guy became a Christian. My friend was transformed, radically changed, radically turned around. He looked at what he'd been and the damage he'd wrought on his family…and he was sorry. The Bible says that godly sorrow brings repentance—a total

180-degree change. This man suffered great sorrow in a godly way for what he'd done to his wife and kids.

He set about trying to turn his family around. With a new Christian perspective in his life, he began taking responsibility. He apologized to his wife and his kids. He was very realistic about his prospects. He didn't go there expecting an overnight sensation and loving arms welcoming him back. All the trust in that family had been broken and it needed to be rebuilt. That takes time.

I know many men who struggle so hard to apologize that, when they do, they think that's it. Everything should be mended, straight away. Sorry, guys. They don't call them "hard yards" because they're easy.

My friend had to spend the next three years living out the fruit of repentance. It wasn't just wishful thinking—"Oh, wouldn't it be nice to have my family back"—it was a complete turnaround in his lifestyle.

Now he's back with his wife and their marriage is phenomenal. The story is not yet over with his kids, but the change has been undeniable. He is no longer a crime figure. He's a father, and his children are being transformed as they come back around.

If your family is off the rails, you can get it back on track. You can, but you are going to have difficulties. It won't be easy, because there's an unshakeable principle in life—you reap what you sow. Your family is off the rails because you're all suffering the consequences of your previous actions. There is a process you can go through, though, to bring your family back from the brink. I am constantly amazed and blessed at seeing how families can, and do, turn around.

Relationship First Aid

In our day–to–day lives we had fallen into the habit of dwelling on the negative.

By now you must have picked up how much I love being married to Beccy. The truth is, though, our marriage was far from great in the first 12 months. I remember getting to the end of our first year and thinking, *"This sucks."* In fact, she would pray I would run off with someone else; I would dream about her dying!

In our day-to-day lives we had fallen into the habit of dwelling on the negative.

One night we went to the drawer and got out our wedding album. We laughed. We cried. We remembered what our honeymoon was like. "This is where we had lobster." We remembered where we stayed and what happened to the car when I forgot to put the cap back on the oil and the whole engine bay was filled with black molasses. (It took me four hours to scrub the stuff off—sorry, Mike!)

We went through all those things and we ended up starting to re-emphasize the good times. In our day-to-day lives we had fallen into the habit of dwelling on the negative, but getting the photos out brought back the good stuff about being together.

The Power of "Remember When..."

"Remember when..." is very powerful because it evokes a whole range of emotional attachments that are more than just memories. Those emotional associations create very positive feelings.

"Wow, yeah, I remember that summer"—it's a memory that triggers off a whole range of emotional responses.

Those emotional responses can actually help you through a bad time. Instead of being victim to a particular bad moment, "Remember when..." can give your family fuel to make it through tough times.

We've even started doing that with the kids: "You know, remember when we did this?" and "Remember when we did that?" It reinforces the highlight times.

I have a photo of my little sister camping with Mom and Dad. It's just one of those photos that floats in my heart, in my being. She's in her swimsuit and I've tied her to a tree. I'm poking her in the belly with a big, long stick. And apparently there was a kookaburra there that used to swoop down just after dinner. So I'd tied my sister to a tree and was putting sausages on her head, trying to get the kookaburra to swoop down and pick them off her head. Mom and Dad caught me doing it, took a photo, and then addressed the issue! But I have this picture of that holiday, which was a highlight of my childhood. When I look at this picture I get a range of very positive emotions about what that particular phase in my life was about.

LEVELING OUT LIFE

We tend to see our life as a collection of emotional highs or lows. As a result, we become focused on whatever particular high or low we're living in right now.

What we should be aware of, though, is that these highs and lows build up to a collective thing called life. Sure, we may be in a trough, but let's fill our trough with emotional "feel-goods." That will level everything out a bit.

CREATE A RELATIONSHIP FIRST AID KIT

I talked about our wedding album, but the ingredients of a relationship first aid kit are probably all over your home. Photo albums are good. Videos are great. Shells from a beach trip, maybe. Something tangible you can hold and say, "Remember when we did this?" and everybody goes, "Yeeaah." We have a family video of the kids doing their "first" things: first walk, first ice-cream, first bike ride.

Preserve those moments in your life by creating a relationship first aid kit, a box of memorabilia. So when you're in the bad times, get the kit out and start going through it. That helps change the tenor of how you're relating. Instead of the problems, these triggers make you remember why you got married. You remember you married your best friend. You'd never met anyone like her. You remember your honeymoon…this date…that outing. So you end up sitting around as a family talking about "Remember when…" and having a wonderful time.

A relationship first aid kit goes very well with a candlelight dinner. Put the kids to bed early. Buy fish and chips or pizza (or something you liked to eat while dating, before you could afford the fancy dinners).

Start talking. "Remember when we did this, honey?" Sometimes wives can get a bit cynical about this sort of thing, particularly if you haven't done it before. But stick at it, keep things light, get her laughing, and let the power of "Remember when…" do its work.

Then, when she does start to open up and laugh about things, look into her eyes. Remember that this is the young girl you married—before the kids, before the mortgage, before the bills, before the challenges. This is the love of your life, your center, your compass.

Remember when…

Creating Character

We've spent our time so far looking at Dad's role in the family, our relationships, and preparing the ground to be a great father.

We've seen that a father is:

1. A man who infuses his own spirit into others.
2. A man who impels and pushes, challenging the mind.
3. The founder of a family—or a society—that is animated by his spirit.

Our responsibility as fathers is an eternal issue. I remember when I first saw my daughter, Jessica. I was overawed that I had just brought an eternal being into the world. Here was the flesh-and-blood vehicle for an eternal spirit!

That really blows out of the water any doubts about what's important in life. What's important is to create *character*.

The poem by Dorothy Law Nolte in the "No Such Thing as a Cookie-Cutter Kid" chapter is a reflection on a universal law that you reap what you sow. We can either scar our children for life or nurture them for life. Unfortunately, our natural tendency as flawed, broken, sinful people is to scar rather than nurture.

As people, we are mostly negative by nature, and a positive, giving worldview is something we have to actively create for ourselves. I don't think any individual grows up completely secure. But a child can grow up valued and confident. I think a child can grow up with an ability to communicate and with a sense of adventure, a sense of being prepared to try something new. I think a child can grow up with an inquisitive mind, with faith in God, and an optimistic outlook on life.

If you are raising your child in an environment of constant criticism, hostility, ridicule, and shame, then you shall reap an insecure and negative child.

But if you create an environment of encouragement, praise, honesty, openness, and trust, then you end up with a much less damaged package: a child who is better prepared to face the world.

So now we're getting down to the nitty-gritty of the job. We've been given an awesome responsibility—creating character in our children.

It's our job to create the internal infrastructure that will support our children through their entire lives. Trying to father a child without addressing the issue of character is like trying to overhaul a car without raising the hood. It might get a nice paint job but it's not going to get very far down the road.

How do we create character? That's the focus of the following chapters.

IT'S FRIGHTENING TO THINK

THAT YOU MARK YOUR

CHILDREN UNFAIR MERELY

BY BEING YOURSELF.

IT SEEMS UNFAIR.

Simone De Beauvoir

GIVE ME THE CHILD UNTIL

THE AGE OF SEVEN AND

I WILL GIVE YOU THE MAN.

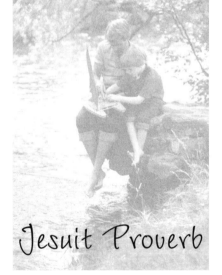

Jesuit Proverb

Monkey See, Monkey Do

I agree with Simone de Beauvoir, but don't be too hard on yourself because you're going to "mark your children." Let's be realistic about the fact that we all damage our children in some way. As parents, as human beings, we can't avoid making mistakes. It's not about trying to be perfect people who produce perfect children. It's about consistently trying to be the very best we can and then passing that on to our kids.

For instance, you don't instruct your children on the decision-making process. Your children *observe* you making decisions and they learn from what they see and hear.

It's very much "monkey see, monkey do." You allow your children to watch you resolve conflict. You allow your children to watch you take responsibility. You allow your children to watch you apologize to your wife and to your friends. You show your children how to ask for forgiveness by apologizing to them when you make a mistake.

I think we naturally do those things, but we have to understand the bigger picture of "monkey see, monkey do." What will your children grow up believing family life is like? If your children just see hostility, verbal arguments, and disagreements at home, they'll grow up believing that's the norm. But if those negatives are just isolated trouble spots in a generally positive family environment, then your children will grow up with a healthy sense of perspective and a positive habit of living out the good stuff.

Some people have said to me: "Parents should never let their children see them have a disagreement." My response to that is: "What planet are you from?!" Sure, I understand their philosophy: if children don't see us argue, they'll have great stability and security in their lives. But I think that if my children can see Beccy and I have a disagreement, then see us resolve it, that breeds far greater security.

It also does something else. It models for our children how to resolve issues. This lesson will be vital to them in future relationships and in marriage. If children have never seen their parents disagree and make up, then how will they know how to deal with disagreement in their own adult lives?

By modeling reconciliation in the way you relate to your own wife, you are sending your children silent positive signals. Your daughters will get the message that, "I want a man who can say he's sorry." Your sons will think: "I want a woman who can forgive." These messages are vital keys to generational success in marriage.

The Most Important Year in a Child's Life

You may have been a father for years and you're thinking: "Am I too late?" After all, you're probably aware of the idea embodied in that old Jesuit proverb: "Give me the child until the age of seven and I will give you the man." Yes, I do think there's a lot of truth in that adage, but I also think that genuine change is possible at any age.

Of course, it's best to start creating character early. If you don't want a brat as a teenager, don't put up with a brat as a 2 year old. If you put in the effort when your children are little, then you've laid a foundation for the rest of your life—a sound relationship. You don't have to spend the next 15 years praying that they leave home because you can't stand them!

So yes, it's best if you create character early.

But...don't despair if you weren't active early and you're only now starting to actively create character. It's true that you'll reap what you sowed; you'll have to hack through the weeds in your child's life for a while.

But if your child is now 15 and you want to start on the track of being a great dad—this is the year to begin. *This year* just became the most important year in your child's life!

If your child is 10 right now and you want to begin creating character, then 10 is your child's most important year.

If your child has just been born, then this is your child's most important year.

See what I'm saying? *Now* is the time when being with your kids is important, when being with your wife is important, when being a family man at the moment is important. Start today.

The most important year in your child's life…is the one they're in right now.

What Kind of Kids Do You Want?

A father's thought*ful*ness or thought*less*ness will be reproduced in his children. Appreciation is something that is taught. If your children don't say please and thank you, it's because you don't.

At a church where Beccy and I were working, we met a young couple who had both been brought up in the whole "free love" environment. They only had one rule: no rules. In terms of their children, this meant "no discipline." Searching for a word to describe those children, only one seems accurate—feral. Feral children. They were *wild*!

It was very tough for that couple. No one else wanted to be around their children; no one wanted to engage with their children; no one wanted to participate with their children.

We had to step this couple through the whole concept of personal discipline. The couple began to understand that discipline is not just about physical discipline. Discipline is about boundaries. It's about teaching children to live within an ordered world that is also occupied by other people.

With this realization came a change in their behavior. They put some boundaries in place. Their children became a lot more manageable, a lot easier, a lot less embarrassing for them, and much less draining. Suddenly their whole circle of friends began to engage with them and their family.

What kind of kids do you want? When people talk about your kids, will it be behind your back or to your face? A lot of couples end up with kids that others talk about behind their back: "I'm not having those people around again." "Did you hear what they said/didn't say?" "Did you hear the way they talk to their parents?" "Did you see what they did to the DVD player?"

So What Kind of Kids *Do* You Want?

Here are two attitudes to think about:

1. RESPECTFUL

    Children have to learn respect for other people. In a sense, that comes out of respect for themselves, but there's a sense of balance to achieve. I think we have to avoid making our kids so egocentric—"I'm number one"—that they forget there's a whole other world out there full of billions of people. They need to respect those people just as they respect themselves. Awareness of the world is a natural part of childhood development, but if they're not trained to see the world as a place full of people who merit respect, they'll never move beyond self-centered behavior.

2. APPRECIATIVE

    Gratitude confirms relationship. Teach your children to say thank you. I really admire the way in some families the children thank their mother for who she is as a person. It's a very affirming thing for Mom. It's wonderful, and if it happens, it's because the father does it.

    I want my kids to become the most polite, appreciative, and respectful people you could wish to meet. The key is this: Get something started in the family and it breaks out into every area of life.

    Take the business world, for instance. If you can close a deal with a thank you and a smile of appreciation, you've won a relationship, not just closed a sale. In business, people skills and social skills take people further than just raw talent for closing a deal.

    These "soft" skills are disappearing from our social landscape. In the future, the people who have those skills are really going to stand out. That's one reason why I'm so keen for my children to be polite, respectful, and appreciative. It's an investment in their future success.

As I said before, you get what you go for with kids. If you tolerate a bratty 2 year old, you're going to get a bratty teenager. If you start instilling appropriate behavior into your youngster, driven by your core values, then that's what you'll get with your teenagers.

If you're the father of a daughter, you may be tempted to say to her mother: "You're her mother, she's your responsibility." Sorry. What your daughter needs and will learn for her life comes as much from you as from her mother.

When you're a dad you literally take out what's in you and you put it in a child. It will either be good or bad. What kind of kids do you want? I'm sure you know. What kind of kids will you get? That's entirely up to you.

Day Care, Night Chaos

Your children are a reflection of who you are. With the hours we work, particularly with the tendency of both parents working away from home, a lot of parents are just too tired to discipline their children. The last thing you want to do at the end of a hard day is come home and discipline your child…even if their behavior is intolerable.

This is especially true if your children have been in day care, as so many children are these days. At day care the children have very few boundaries placed on them. At the end of the day when you pick them up and you want to have good times with them, you definitely don't want to come across as an ogre. So it's very easy to continue that boundary-free approach the day care people use.

The problem is not with the child. It's with us. In our culture, our working life drains our emotional tank. We've made the career decision that everything else comes ahead of our family, so by the end of the day we're spent.

The first thing you have to get right is your emotional tank. Make sure there's enough in your tank to give your kids what they need from you.

ATTENTION SEEKERS, LOVE NEEDERS

When I say "need," I mean their genuine need, when they're in balance. I don't mean the "need for attention" that afflicts many children today. You know what I mean. You've seen them: kids who seem to have a constant need for attention. They don't seem to care what kind of attention it is, either. They'll behave badly just so they can be in the center of your frame.

Should we give these bratty kids the awful "attention" they "need"?

No, because it's not attention they really need. What they need is more love and affection from their parents. That's their central need. That's their *real* need.

In my experience, this hole develops in the preschool years. Dad, it can be filled with love and affection from your well-charged emotional tank. After that, the school years are very manageable.

So the first thing to get right is *your* emotional tank. Make sure there's enough in there to give your kids the care they need when the day caregivers have finished for the day.

Fabulous Fathers Can Be Deadly Dads

Try to see things from your child's perspective. They may be *little* people, but they are still people. As dads we're dealing with little lives. Little people don't get treated the same as big people, but they should still be treated as people.

You see, a fabulous father to one child can be a deadly dad to another. In the Bible, David was a fabulous father toward his son Solomon. Yet he exerted an absolutely deadly influence on another son, Absalom. Solomon went on to fulfill David's promises...but Absalom destroyed David's kingdom!

INVESTMENT VERSUS REJECTION

Can we tell the difference in David's approach to the two boys? Fortunately, the Bible is very clear about the difference. The Bible describes David *instructing* Solomon. It also says that David never corrected Absalom in any way, shape, or form. David invested in Solomon but left Absalom bereft, rejected, and directionless.

I believe that the outcomes of David's kids—Solomon and Absalom —were very much the responsibility of their father.

We have to be *active* in the lives of all our children.

No Such Thing as a Cookie-Cutter Kid

Your children won't appreciate the wisdom of what you do as a father. They don't realize that it is for their future you're applying boundaries, instilling values, and setting standards. So if you see something you don't like about your child's behavior, you're the one who has to develop a sensitive strategy for changing it. You have to tailor your message to the character of the child.

You have to tailor your message to the character of the child.

A friend of mine Ian Woods had a son who had become obsessed with the issue of peer acceptance. I mean obsessed. It was all he talked about, yelled about, and carried on about. He was impossible about it.

Every child is desperate to be accepted by their peers, so as adults we often find ourselves doing things that embarrass our children. If this seems to be happening all the time, though, then your child probably has an issue with acceptance and rejection. Don't pander to it. Get the stumbling block out of the way in a way that's sensitive to the nature of the particular child. You have to tailor your message to the character of the child.

Because Ian's youngest son was so wrapped up in what his peers thought and was embarrassed about his family, his dad provided the boy with a lesson in perspective, a reality check. The dad put on some short pants, long socks that came up past his knees, a white T-shirt, and knotted a handkerchief on his head. He pulled his pants way up over his waist, up nearly under his armpits. Then he stood at the school bus stop and waved goodbye to his son, who was totally humiliated.

When the son got home, they had a pointed discussion about what happened. "Son, if you're going to be such a dweeb about this, I'll make an issue of it until it goes away. You have to learn that family comes first!" It was a short, sharp, listen-and-learn experience that was just right for that particular boy. Not right for every kid, but Ian knew his son and he had to do something to put his boy back on track. The kind of children he wanted to raise were not ones who were embarrassed about their mom and dad.

That was the right strategy for the youngest son. What about the middle son who was a very sensitive, talented, creative person? There's no way my friend would do anything to embarrass the middle son. The youngest one, though, could take it.

Each child is different. There's no such thing as cookie-cutter kids. We have to deal with each child in the way that is uniquely appropriate to them.

With my own kids, I know that Noah responds to one kind of discipline, and Jessica to another. Kids are like that. Kids need that. They're little people and none is identical.

In Dad's Image

A gentleman I met at one of our training seminars talked to me about how he deeply regretted not acknowledging the uniqueness of his children. He was a very successful business manager and consultant. He worked as a top global executive for one of the world's leading computing companies. He was an acknowledged expert in organizational human resources—a people person if ever there was one. But he had a shadow over his family, because he treated all his kids the same.

He had five kids, four of them boys. Every Sunday morning, every one of those boys was dressed up exactly like his dad, with identical pants and bow ties. Off they marched to church. For three of the boys this was fine, but the fourth was a rogue. He was a messy, woolly-haired, wild-and-free sort of character. He wasn't undisciplined. He wasn't rebellious. He was just...different.

His shirt wouldn't stay tucked in, his pants always seemed out of place and his hair never sat right. He wasn't happy in the bow tie "box." Dad's reaction? He continually forced the child into that box.

As the son grew older, he did everything he could to break out of the confining box. His friendship with his father became distant. He felt as though he never measured up or made his dad happy.

In reality, that was far from the truth, but such is the power of perception—what we perceive is what we believe. If your child thinks they don't fit, they won't. If they think they are unloved/unattractive/unwelcome, the results will be just the same as if all those things were true.

This dad, a great human being, had fallen for the temptation of parental convenience and ease. It was easier to try to get his son to conform to his own likeness than to let him be his own unique self.

It reminds me of a principle I've seen at work in every kind of connection between human beings, at every level of society: *Rules without relationship lead to rebellion.*

If a child lives with criticism, she learns to condemn.

If a child lives with hostility, she learns to fight.

If a child lives with ridicule, she learns to be shy.

If a child lives with shame, she learns to feel guilty.

If a child lives with encouragement, she learns confidence.

If a child lives with praise, she learns to appreciate.

If a child lives with approval, she learns to like herself.

If a child lives with acceptance and friendship, she learns to find love in the world.

Dorothy Law Nolte

PART

2

Raising

Kids

The Way He Should Go

"Train up a child in the way he should go, and when he is old he will not turn from it" (Proverbs 22:6).

One of the miracles of families is how two parents can produce genuinely different children. That uniqueness is something every child deserves (and needs) to have valued. Some have misinterpreted this verse to mean *discipline* a child so they become a certain sort of person. In reality, however, it means to *identify the gifts* that are in a child and then raise the child in the context of those gifts, to help the child discover the destiny that grows from his or her own uniqueness. In turn, this will set a path for the child's life.

As parents we have a responsibility to find what is good in each of our children's lives.

A business associate of ours had three boys who were each very different. As these boys grew, the eldest two naturally found their place in life and the family. Their gifts and personalities blossomed. One was good at percussion. One was good with guitars. But the youngest son (from the time he turned 8 to when he reached 12 years old) could not find a place of belonging that was uniquely his own. He was musically talented like his brothers, but he still didn't feel he belonged.

My friend responded by pursuing a range of activities with his son, trying to find something in which his son was able to say, "Dad, I'm good at this." Nothing seemed to fit. Everyone—especially children that age—has a natural tendency to compare and compete with others. So the fact that this boy just didn't shine in any of these activities really exacerbated the situation.

But my friend persevered. After trying many different things over several years, he finally found the answer when he got his son up on a horse. Horse riding! Something so different from the musical bent of the rest of the family. Something so unexpected. Something uniquely his own. A passion he could share with his father.

The passion for riding only lasted a few years, but it helped establish self-confidence in this child, and on the basis of that confidence, the young man began to pursue *the way he should go*—a unique path destined exclusively for him.

Find the way each of your kids should go. It probably won't be the same for each. Work with them to find the right path and set them on it.

To *"train up a child in the way he should go"* means that you are preoccupied with your child fulfilling his or her own destiny, not reliving yours.

If you get them started in the right direction toward self-confidence and self-fulfillment, they will not depart from it.

Six Keys to Raising Kids

The following are six keys to raising kids. It's not a formula, but rather elements I have seen work and we have personally used successfully.

1. Have an affectionate and affirming relationship.

    Growing children is like growing young plants. Every word we say is an opportunity to frame and shape their world. The most crucial thing you can do is speak words of affirmation and affection into their life from the time of their conception.

    Be positive. And don't allow your kids to be negative, even though that's the way we all naturally tend to be. If your child speaks negatively about themselves, correct them, lovingly and firmly. Don't let it pass. The girl who's allowed to say she looks ugly will grow up believing it.

    What causes children to act and think that way? They're simply repeating the kind of worldview they receive from other people. Watch your words. Do you call yourself fat? Does your wife say she's unattractive?

    Instead, affirm and compliment your wife's appearance...and do the same for your children.

    When my son Noah was young, he went through a stage when he stopped eating his food and would get really upset after meals. We had hurt him by commenting on the "pokey-out belly" he had when he ate. We thought it was cute, but he interpreted our comments and fond laughter as a judgment that he was ugly. How old was he? 12? 14? No. He was just 3 years old!

This really upset us and caused us to be attentive to what we said and how we said it. For our son, that could have been the start of an unhealthy association with food and a damaging eating disorder. The wonderful thing about children is that they bend but don't break—just like young plants you can train to climb a trellis. Through our affection and affirmation we were able to correct our mistake and Noah's perception of his belly. Children are very forgiving of our mistakes! They give us the grace to learn and grow as parents.

2. Be open communicators.

    Talk about anything, at any time. Continually communicate. I make Jessica tell me about her day. When she says, "Dad, I can't remember," I stop and *make* her tell me.

    I insist that the channels of communication are open. I've done that since she could talk, because I want the channels to still be open when she is 20.

    As parents we have to deliberately train and equip our children with the tools to express their emotions. If I am concerned about something they have done, I don't just tell them it is wrong. I sit them down and say something like: "Sweetheart, I am feeling a little upset about something you said/did and I need to talk about it." I have done this since Jessica began talking, even *before* she could understand. Now, years later, if she is upset, she says, "Dad, I need to talk to you about something that is upsetting me." Give your child their tools *before they need them* so they can draw on them in times of need.

3. Communicate clearly and specifically about sex.

    Make sex normal. It's a normal, powerful, natural thing. Sociologists tell us that human beings have three major drives: food, shelter, and sex. We talk to our children about money. We talk to them about caring for their home. We need to talk to them about their sexuality. It's going to hit them one day and they need to be able to talk openly with us. Once again, give them the tools to cope before they need them.

    We also have to prepare our children for a world that is preoccupied with sex. The Bible calls it lasciviousness, or a preoccupation with lewd sexual behavior; and sure enough, the world is preoccupied with sex.

The Bible also talks about modesty, and that's something we seem to have forgotten in Western church culture. Let me put it to you in straight talk: we are not meant to dress, act, talk, dance, or joke in any way that could be seen as a provocative sexual "come on." That is lasciviousness. When you're with your wife, go for it. That's pure. But around your children, or allowing your kids to act out, dress, or behave in a sexual manner, is not acceptable.

All children—boys and girls alike—need to be prepared for this challenge. There is a statistic to the effect that 45 percent of all pornography accessed on the Internet is viewed by women. It's hard to believe, but it points to a change in our society. I've seen this change myself, in what we do. The sexualization of our society has affected both genders. With so many sleazy messages around for our children to imbibe, it's important that Dad is always an approachable (and proactive) source of good, clean wisdom on the subject of sex. It is not your wife's job to have "the talk." Both your daughter and son need to get a balanced, wholesome male perspective as well.

4. Be a good role model.

Where there's no model, there's a vacuum, and it will be filled. When "moral America" was decrying Marilyn Manson for his satanic and aggressively vulgar music, he said something to the effect that "if you will not raise your children, I will." Powerful point. You have to be a role model for your children and you have to be a good one. The most powerful influences children will ever have are their parents. Please, don't choose to abrogate your responsibility by transferring it to the school, church, or sports coach. It's not their responsibility; it's yours.

5. Stay tuned in to their world.

Always be aware of what your children are feeding themselves—their music, their friends, their movies, their life. Go to a movie with them. Watch the cartoons on TV. Read a book before you let them read it. Listen to their music—stop, listen, and read the lyrics. If your child is depressed, it may be because they're listening to songs with suicidal lyrics. Find out what they're plugging into their ego. You'll have to take responsibility for setting limits on it, too. Control that stuff.

If ever there was a "home invader," it's the TV. A parent said to me recently, "We have a television in all the bedrooms and our son always goes to sleep with it on—it's a great babysitter."

Well, what is little Johnny going to sleep with between the hours of 7:30 and 9:30 at night? It ranges from hard-sell advertisements to programs full of sexual and violent behaviors. You are giving this invited, non-regulated "guest" permission to enter your family and feed your children whatever garbage a pervert producer deems fit for so-called "adult" programming.

If your children watch TV two or three hours every night, that adds up to 14 to 21 hours each week. This box-shaped "guest" invades and influences the behavior and morality of your children—the internet is another familiar "guest" these days. Add 30 hours a week of school teachers and school kids and you have up to 51 hours of external influences on your children. How many hours per week of wholesome, loving parental influence do they get to balance out the others? It's your responsibility to set limits and be consistent about them.

6. Pray for your children and yourself.

It's vital that dads take spiritual responsibility by praying for their kids, their marriage, and their life. You should be constantly asking God for His protection over your family. He'll listen. He'll respond. It is absolutely vital.

If you don't know how to ask God's favor on your family and friends, give us a call. We'll put you in touch with someone who will help. I cannot overstress the importance of a father praying for his family. When Dad's praying, Heaven moves and hell shuts up!

One thing I'm constantly surprised by is the myth that women are more spiritual than men. People who make these sorts of comments must think the Bible is complete fiction. The Bible is predominantly about the spiritual journeys of *men* as they battle to establish the Kingdom of God and redeem their families.

God created you, a man, first, because He wanted to establish a divine order—you in close relationship with Him, prepared and equipped to take care of the family He has given you. Christ is Prophet, Priest, and King to the Church. A father is the same thing to his family.

Don't Do It, Dad

Balancing the six dos of parenting are three definite don'ts.

1. Don't burden them.

   With knowledge comes responsibility. Children don't have life knowledge, so don't burden them with life's responsibilities. They don't need to know about the state of your marriage, your job, or your finances—unless they can make a contribution and help resolve the situation. But most kids can't. They're just kids. Don't tell them money's tight; that makes them carry responsibility for family debt. Don't tell them you are having marriage problems, because they can't help you solve them.

   But short-term gain can bring long-term pain.

   Many single parents really struggle to maintain this kind of discretion in communication with their child. They are at home with their child, with no adult companions. Naturally, they want someone to turn to and discuss life's issues, battles, and victories. The closest person at hand is their child.

   But short-term gain can bring long-term pain. When you're tempted to enjoy the gratification of sharing your life's troubles with your child, that's the time to *delay gratification*. Find an adult friend.

Some people disagree with me on this. They say I'm trying to shelter children from life's realities. They're right. I am. It's great to expose your child to life-changing, life-enhancing experiences. However, there's a big difference between that and burdening them with life's battles and conflicts.

2. Don't break a promise.

    Consistency is the "golden rule" of child discipline. Don't change the rules on them. Consistency brings security and boundaries to their world. When they know the rules, they feel the freedom, safety, and protection to move at will within those boundaries.

    A child doesn't know the difference between a broken promise and a lie.

    A child will start collecting their bucket and spade as soon as you promise to take them to the beach. If you forget, if you decide you can't be bothered, if you just change your mind, or if you allow a work commitment to constantly interrupt your dedicated time, then you devalue your word and teach your child you cannot be trusted.

    There is a difference between that and unforeseen circumstances, and a habit of broken promises will convince your children that lying is a natural part of life.

    Renegotiating your arrangement is not the same as breaking a promise. I've had to renegotiate many times. This isn't bad—it teaches flexibility and helps us model grace to each other. But if I commit to taking my daughter to breakfast and suddenly a meeting comes up, I don't break my promise. I reschedule our date. And I keep it.

    Let your "yes" be "yes" and your "no" be "no." You don't have to cater to your child's every whim. If you don't want to do something, simply don't agree to it. But if you do agree to it, make sure you demonstrate that you're a man of your word.

3. Don't put up with it.

    As a parent you may be struggling to find a replacement for the inadequate models that shaped your own life. So you look around at friends and peers to see how they do things, to see what their advice is. However, just because something may be acceptable behavior in one family doesn't make it right for yours. Raise your children to be adults you will be proud of, rather than embarrassments.

As mentioned previously if you tolerate rude, spiteful behavior in a child at 3, you'll have to put up with it at 13. If you tolerate a tantrum-throwing child, you'll inherit a whining, tantrum-throwing teenager. Do you think it's acceptable for a 40 year old to throw himself to the floor in anger because they don't like their birthday cake? If it's not acceptable for a 40 year old, don't accept it from your 4 year old. It's a lot easier to stop inappropriate behavior early on...and you'll be saving your child from a very embarrassing scene at their 40th birthday party!

With kids, you get what you go for.

We never had the "terrible twos," because we decided we wouldn't put up with it. At the first sign of it, we made it clear we wouldn't tolerate it. You get what you go for, particularly if you go for it promptly and early on.

The idea for this strategy came from a great friend Bobbie Houston. Bobbie told us she simply made the decision that her children would not experience the "terrible twos." She said, "Why should two years old be the most terrible time? That's supposed to be the most fun time of their life." As a result, her children didn't go through that stage. When people talked to Bobbie about how rebellious children can be, particularly teenagers, Bobbie simply refused to believe that paradigm. So they never experienced the rebellious teenage years. They didn't believe it, they didn't go looking for it, they didn't have it, and they didn't tolerate it.

You have to do your own growing, no matter how tall your grandfather was.

Irish Proverb

The Rites of Passage

Develop family rites of passage for each important stage of your children's development and growth. These will become the hallmarks and milestones of their lives.

I keep a journal for my children. I've done so since their conception. It's just a very small thing I do every now and again. I made an entry when they first took a step, when they first spoke, and their first day of school. Their first airplane ticket is stuck in there. I'll keep doing it, too: first trip to Disneyland; first trip to the movies; their first Bible.

Years from now, they'll cast their eyes over these things and get the sense of a developing life. These events are the rites of passage that every family should celebrate.

BENCHMARK THE HALLMARKS

Maturity is not about age; it's about the acceptance of responsibility. During their childhood your child needs *you* to benchmark the key events that are the hallmarks of growth, maturity, and responsibility:

- ❖ Responsibility for money.
- ❖ Responsibility for getting dressed.
- ❖ Responsibility for tidying their room.
- ❖ Responsibility for being prepared for school.
- ❖ Responsibility for graduating.

In a book called *Raising a Modern-day Knight*, author Robert Lewis points out the dour realization that in our Western world we don't have rites of passage such as in other cultures. So he and his friends set about creating their own rites of passage. Once a year these four fathers and their sons go away to camp. They pick a time for these camps aligned with a key event in their sons' lives, like entering preschool, starting high school, or approaching the age for dating, etc.

They go away at these times as a rite of passage and talk through the upcoming challenges at the same time: "This is how you deal with it," "This is what the girl thing is about," and "This is what the sex thing is about." They established clear milestones in their sons' lives. I don't think there are better people to set a child's milestones than the child's own parents—if they're attentive, tuned in, and actually focused on their child's development.

If you are an attentive father, you can turn an adolescent's embarrassment into the proud moment of an emerging adult. Many of us still flush with embarrassment at the times we stumbled through the defining moments of our emerging adulthood. Many a man cringes at the memory of his voice breaking. Don't let that happen to your son. Prepare him for this change of life. Get him buzzed about the fact that when it happens it marks the onset of his masculinity.

Then, when it happens, celebrate it with him in a dignified, mature way. It will be a rite of passage for him, a hallmark of maturity—not fuel for toilet humor at school.

What about doing something on his 13th birthday? Go and buy a razor with him. Sit him down and show him how to shave. Go to a menswear store by yourself and get a professional lesson in how to tie a necktie correctly...then teach it to your boy.

It's the same for your little girl. Some ladies only have horrific memories of their first period. But if you treat your daughter to a special dinner and a new dress when this happens, it will engrave on her spirit the notion that her womanhood is a treasure of great value—something unique and special.

Or if you think the time is right for her to go out on a date ("May that day never come," I hear an army of men roar as they remember what they were like!), *then you take her out yourself!*

It's a rite of passage: a model date with Dad. Daddy models how a man should act, what a man should say and what a man should do. Daddy opens the door, Daddy seats her first, and Daddy pays the bill.

Daddy is polite, gets her home on time, is dressed nicely, drives safely et cetera, et cetera. If you raise the bar, if you increase her expectations, if you benchmark the experience for her, then she won't settle for less.

These are the important progressions from childhood to adulthood. Make every rite of passage a positive one: "This is a new change in your life. Isn't it great!" See these times as opportunities to come together, not grow apart.

Fathers Are Fun

Have Fun With Your Kids

Life is an adventure that needs to be lived. It's the same with fathering. I think we have made fatherhood sound too serious. Your kids just want to have fun. Give them what they want. Here are some ways that fun dads can get the most out of each stage of their kids' childhood. Even if you're busy with a career, there's still plenty of time to get involved.

Newborn to Crawling

Bath times are great. Blow bubbles on their belly. Tickle them. Feeding times can be really fun times. Life at this stage is all about segments: five minutes, ten minutes, fifteen minutes. Grab some segments of baby's day and have some fun.

They will interact most with their mother at this stage. But if you do not discipline yourself to get involved early, you'll find it more difficult later in their life.

Pre-walking

Crawl with them. That's right. Lie down on the floor and crawl with them. Let them crawl over you.

They'll love it if you get down to their level to be with them, banging balls on tables and floors. Start to wrestle and play. You'll notice their personality emerge. You'll see what frustrates them and how they deal with problems. You'll start to develop a matrix of understanding to draw on in later years.

WALKING TO PRESCHOOL

At this age it's all about colors, coloring, lots of paint, mess and mud, running and tumbling, and kicking balls.

This is when you start reading with them. Sit with them and get them started. Show them how to sit down and quietly read. It's so much better than just having the DVD or TV playing all the time in the background. Read them a story before they go to bed, even if it's just pointing at the pictures. But realize that what you're doing is teaching them the value of books and getting them into the very rewarding habit of reading. Since our kids were 3 years old we put them to bed with books. Now, later in life, they put themselves to bed with books.

EARLY SCHOOL

This is when you start interacting with them and their friends. It's a time of outdoor activities, sports, kiddie farms, flying kites, fairs, and festivals.

You also get involved in their wonderful world of imagination. Build them a tent underneath the coffee table, or a tent in the backyard for the weekend. If it's raining, put the tent up in the family room. Or move the TV and DVD player into the kids' room for a day and spend the whole rainy weekend in bed eating with them, cooking, and watching movies. This stage is about quantity time, not quality time. The more they get, the more they want. So give it to them. You don't have them under your roof forever.

8 TO 14 YEARS OF AGE

This is usually an age when sports and/or physical activities are important, so go along, watch them, and encourage them.

Actively seek things they're interested in. Help them excel at those things.

Find positive anchors for your child's self-esteem.

Dad and daughter having dates; Dad and son having dates: take them out and model appropriate behavior.

Find positive anchors for your child's self-esteem.

Volunteer as a weekly coach for your child's local sports team. With sports or activities, it doesn't matter what they choose; just find something your child enjoys and then encourage them. If it's reading, encourage them to be a reader. If it's a sport, encourage them to play. If it's music, encourage them to get loud.

This is the time to find positive anchors for your child's self-esteem. At this age their eyes are moving outward from their family toward the wider world. So in a world full of negativity, you need to find a beacon of light for them to focus on. Help them find something they can be good at and enjoy with your support.

The Five "A"s of Adolescence

We want our children to grow up healthy and heterosexual. This means we have to define for them the meaning of healthy sexuality. A sexually whole human being is secure, not emotionally dependant or driven.

Let me preface the five "A"s of adolescence by saying that children get their identity from their father and sense of security from their mother. Nurturing, security, and comfort come from mom; their identity comes from dad. If a child has a corrupted view of dad, they'll have a corrupted view of their own identity, and that's where a distortion of sexuality can come from.

So when your child reaches adolescence, these five "A"s are very important. These are the five stages of sexual development, the five stages of an adolescent's interpersonal development:

- ❖ AWARENESS
- ❖ ATTRACTION
- ❖ APPRECIATION
- ❖ ANXIETY
- ❖ ACCEPTANCE

1. AWARENESS.

   They become aware of their own body. A child wakes up with an erection, a wet dream, a sexual fantasy. It's all a by-product of their age, their hormones. Your role is to help your child understand the profound forces that are at work in them. They'll need your help to come to terms with these powerful and disturbing new impulses. Don't allow any room for shame to creep in. Shame corrupts and kills. Gently help your child learn to benchmark their burgeoning sexual awareness alongside and within the context of your family's values.

2. ATTRACTION.

They start to get attracted to the opposite sex. Your job is to help them see past mere attraction. They need to be able to define the difference between love and lust.

Love is wanting to satisfy others, at the expense of self. Love desires to give. Lust is wanting to satisfy self, at the expense of others. Lust desires to get.

So we have to encourage our kids, who quite naturally are self-centered, to make the step to the next level.

3. APPRECIATION.

This is when someone genuinely values the person they find attractive. The first two "A"s will happen without our help: Adolescents naturally become sexually aware and they develop attractions. But *appreciation* happens at a higher level and we have to help our children reach for it. If we as dads can help our child make a strong distinction between sexual attraction and appreciation, we'll be blessing our child with a very positive basis for their future relationship. Sex then becomes the most intimate form of a shared appreciation within the bounds of a loving, committed relationship—marriage. It is not something you try to take from someone you don't care about.

4. ANXIETY.

This is such a big thing for an adolescent—high anxiety about "who I am," "how do I look," "what do I weigh," and "what should I wear." They're looking for a basis for their sense of self-worth and their place in the world. That's deep stuff. There's no point addressing the symptoms ("Oh, you look fine, honey"); you have to address the root of it by helping your child find wholeness within themselves and within their community.

The time to start establishing a healthy self-esteem is in the early years, not their teenage years. Affirm them as clever, strong, handsome, beautiful, funny, and creative before they can even understand the concepts.

5. ACCEPTANCE.

Adolescence is a time when a child is in turmoil and they have a terrible dread that people are able to look right through them and see what is going on inside. That's why peer acceptance is so important to them. They would "just die" if anyone knew the truth—the truth that they're a valuable person experiencing the onset of adulthood.

The same strategy for dealing with *anxiety* applies here: healthy doses of affection and affirmation. All adolescents want to move away from *anxiety* to *acceptance*. Most of them choose to seek external acceptance by dressing, speaking, and acting in ways that are acceptable in their chosen peer group. Our role is to steer them toward a different kind of *acceptance*. We have to help move our children from *anxiety* into *self-acceptance*. *Self-acceptance* is the hallmark of a mature person.

MY FATHER WAS AN AMAZING
MAN. THE OLDER I GOT,
THE SMARTER HE GOT.

Mark Twain

Protecting Your Children...
From Their Friends

In high school I was great friends with "Eric." Eric was very popular, very outgoing. The members of his family were well known for their roguish nature...and Eric was just like them. He wasn't a bad kid; just a wild kid from a wild home. One day after school, my mom and dad sat me down and destroyed my 13-year-old world. They said I was not allowed to be Eric's friend any more.

It was a bombshell. I was shattered. But it was also one of the most strategic decisions my parents ever made for me. They told me my friendship with Eric was over. They told Eric's parents, too. They even told the school that they did not want me associating with this guy.

They met with the teachers and reviewed class seating arrangements. They went at it really hard and made it impossible for me to stay friends with Eric. They broke the relationship on my behalf.

Six months later, Eric was killed by a lethal mix of a stolen motorbike and his father's alcohol. He had just become a teenager when it happened—that could have been me.

When my parents actively broke that friendship, it did much more than take me away from a dangerous friend. It shifted my life and my behavior onto a completely different track. Instead of being associated with the tragic lifestyle that led Eric to an early death, I'd been set on a whole new path that bore positive fruit.

As parents we have a responsibility and *a right* to choose our children's friends and facilitate positive relationships until our children are old enough to make appropriate and wise judgments of their own.

Think Inside the Box

Our calling as parents and fathers is to raise our children in the way they should go. This means digging out the best that is in them and helping facilitate their dreams and find their future. The associations our children make are an important part of that. In the first part of our children's lives, we need to box them inside positive relationships.

You know it's true: *birds of a feather flock together*. Bad company corrupts good morals.

Bad character, bad morals, negative activities: they all congregate together. With peer groups, it also works the other way: good character, strong morals, positive influences. We can actively help develop positive peer groups around our children and in their lives.

Who do they vacation with? What sort of movies are they watching? What inputs are they receiving? What sort of music do they listen to? What topics do they discuss? What kind of language do they use?

I think you need to be very insistent on this aspect of parenting. Some of my friends have always made a point of being very strong about their children's associations. For instance, when it comes to childcare, there are only one or two people they trust to babysit their children.

Before Beccy and I had kids of our own, I thought these friends of ours were fanatical, ludicrous even. But years later, when we look at their children, we can see the great results this approach produced. Their boys are caring, smart, compassionate young men. And now, even at a young adult age, they are trusted to do what they want and travel anywhere because their core values have been firmly set for life. The work is done, because mom and dad were very careful about whom the boys were allowed to interact with at an early age.

You can create a positive environment, not just for your own children but for their friends, too. Make your home and your presence a place where your children's friends feel welcome. Make room in your life for your children's friends. That way your own children will be around home and around you a lot more often. And your positive impact on your children's friends may well save the life of a great kid like Eric.

Encourage and Nurture

Teach your kids to love themselves, praise themselves, believe in themselves, and discipline themselves.

Believe in your children. Praise your children. Encourage your children. So when the world tries to tell them they're ugly or dumb, they can say, "That's not true. My Dad said I'm the best and most beautiful in the whole wide world."

Make your home a sanctuary of dreams and visions—a place where everything is possible, where all dreams may come true, where all adventures are real, where crocodiles are wrestled before bedtime, mountains are conquered—a place where elephants brush their teeth and teddy bears talk.

The Best Green Blob in the World

I believe that one of my responsibilities as a father is to know my child so well that I will help that child find their gifting, their talent. I'll help them find it and then help send them on their way.

I remember when Jessica started coming home from school with artwork. She'd say, "Daddy, look at this. This is great." And I'd say, "Yes, it is, baby. It's really good." And that's the start of it: affirming her feeling that she's done something really well. "Oh, Jessica Jane, that is the most incredible large orange blob on white paper I've ever seen!" So when she comes home two days later, or two months later, she's telling me, "Daddy, look at this. This is the best green blob in the world!"

Your kids will progress from green blobs to models, planes, projects, cars, and university degrees. But their world will be rock-solid if they always have a dad who says, "Yeah, you've done great."

No Second-hand Dreams

My child is not me. I have to be aware of that. Just because I may have wanted to be something in particular doesn't mean my child will want to follow that dream. I may have dreamed of being a great tennis player, a great salesman, a great preacher, or a great businessman, but my child may not share my dreams. Some children do not want to go into dad's business.

A dad's notion of his kids inheriting the family dream is very self-focused. Our focus should be to nurture and encourage our children's dreams and desires, whatever they are. Sure, there are many great examples of children following in their father's footsteps...for multiple generations. But in general, our kids' footsteps lead in other directions. If your child has dreams that are different from yours, you have to give them the freedom and encouragement to pursue them.

NOT LIKE A VIRGIN

Having said that, it's important you insert boundaries into your encouragement—like graphite rods inserted in a nuclear reactor to stop the reaction from getting out of control.

In his book, *Losing My Virginity*, Richard Branson, the business maverick behind Virgin Airlines, Virgin Records, and Virgin "You Name It," talks about smuggling records in and out of Brussels to avoid paying VAT (Value Added Tax) in England. He was caught by the Customs Department and spent a night or two in jail. He remembers lying on the cell cot thinking: "All my life I have broken the rules and all my life I have thought that rules were for breaking." He realized, there in jail, that there are consequences for actions. He made the decision that he would never again engage in a business practice that would end up embarrassing him or putting him back in a situation like that. He says there were many times in his later business years when he could have bent or broken the rules, but the resolve he made in jail helped him through.[1]

What's very telling is that Branson talks about how his parents encouraged him to break rules when he was younger.

They never taught him to balance personal goals with social responsibility. They didn't give him any "graphite rods." So Branson had to learn about boundaries for himself, in jail. Of course, a couple of nights in a cell isn't such a high price to pay to learn a valuable lesson in ethics. But it could have been a lot worse, and we don't want our children to have to pay a higher price to learn to insert healthy boundaries in their personal lives.

Branson honors his parents for nurturing his entrepreneurial outlook on life, but there were other aspects of their parenting style that got him into trouble. Our role as dads is to give our kids the encouragement to dream and achieve but to also make sure they realize there are two sides to the coin.

NURTURE A POSITIVE SPIRIT

Your kids will model what you teach them. They're sponges. Be aware that you're teaching them all the time! I can tell my kids to respect people, but what really teaches them respect is seeing me put those words into action by respecting other people.

So if I see my daughter disrespecting someone, I have to look back and ask: "Where did she learn that?" "Have I actually been modeling respect?" Maybe she was with me in the car when I was complaining about someone…maybe that's where she learned disrespect and negativity? Children are always watching, listening, and learning. And that's great—they're so open to being encouraged and nurtured, directed, and corrected.

ENDNOTE

1. Richard Branson, *Losing My Virginity*, (NY: Three Rivers Press, 1998).

Physical Affection — Kids Need It; Don't Fear It

KIDS NEED CUDDLES

A kid is not a car. You can't just grease and oil a child every 1,500 miles and hope it's all done. Kids need constant physical attention. Physical contact and touch with their father or mother will make all the difference to a child.

You might buy them a soft toy and think that does it, but remember your children's emotional needs. A free cuddle does more than an expensive soft toy.

Why does a cuddle meet emotional needs? There's the security of being held. When a child comes for a cuddle and is accepted, they experience something wonderful: the complete opposite of rejection.

Then there's the surety and purity of sitting on daddy's lap and knowing it's a wholesome, clean physical encounter.

That sets the blueprint for your children's reactions to other men. Wholesome contact from Dad is a positive signpost to their healthy and whole heterosexual development.

SURETY AND PURITY OF A FATHER'S LOVE

I remember going to the house of a friend of mine whose daughter was going through a challenging stage as a young teenager. The family was sitting watching TV, and there was his little girl, who was struggling to be a young lady, curled up on her daddy's lap, having a cuddle and nestling time. It was an amazing thing to see.

Some guys get really uncomfortable with that scenario. They feel really self-conscious interacting with their blossoming daughters. They pull back. But if a girl can't get positive, non-sexual physical attention at home, she'll go somewhere else for physical affirmation. And you know what form that will take.

So why are we so uncomfortable about physical touch between fathers and daughters? Isn't it sad that a tiny bunch of perverts have managed to influence the psyche of entire nations of well-balanced men? The fear of being accused of pedophilia is a pervasive one these days.

As a result, men hold back from being physically intimate with their children. They're afraid they'll be accused of being a child abuser. Or they're actually scared they may become one! A tide of fear has swept over our culture, interfering with a dad's wonderful capacity to love through being physically attentive to his kids.

Guys, there's nothing wrong with clean, wholesome touch.

Guys, there's nothing wrong with clean, wholesome touch. In a world that's full of perversion and pornography, our children deserve to experience whole, sound, non-sexual touching from their fathers. If your children don't have that, if there's a lack of whole, sound, non-sexual touching from Dad, then when they go looking for touch and affection from someone else, the experience will end up unsound, sexual, and non-affirming.

The irony is that many dads back off at the exact time a girl most needs wholesome affirmation from her father. She hits puberty, her breasts start to form, she begins menstruating, and her hormones are wild. Dad gets uncomfortable because his little girl is turning into a woman, but that's the time when she needs to know that *touch can be non-sexual.*

Men have to be in tune with reality on this one. There is a lot of sexual abuse going on out there. Don't take what I've said as an excuse to just ignore society's feelings on this issue. Don't give anyone reason to accuse you of improper behavior. There are plenty of opportunities to show physical affection in a family setting where you're not alone. Remember, people don't usually accuse men of abuse because they want to cause trouble. They care about the children involved. So balance your children's need for physical affection with the need to be above reproach. Keep your physical intimacy out in the open, not behind closed doors.

THE POSITION OF THE FATHER

IS THE THANKLESS PROVIDER

FOR ALL, AND THE ENEMY OF ALL.

J. August Strindberg

EVERY MOTHER GENERALLY HOPES THAT

HER DAUGHTER WILL SNAG A BETTER

HUSBAND THAN SHE MANAGED TO——BUT

SHE'S CERTAIN THAT HER BOY WILL NEVER

GET AS GREAT A WIFE AS HIS FATHER DID.

John King

The Majority of Men— Healthy & Wholesome

One of the most heartbreaking things I've ever experienced took place when I was running a Wednesday after-school youth meeting for our local church. There was the sweetest little girl who attended every week. But every week after the meeting, she'd go home and her mother would sexually abuse her. She was caught in a terrible emotional place because she was beginning to develop sexually. As a result, she was starting to enjoy the sexual interaction. This created a powerful cycle of guilt for her.

We tried to do something about it. If she'd been abused by a man, it would have been easy to deal with, but because it was her mother, we found it very difficult. People didn't want to believe us. We told the school. We told the entire range of people we were supposed to tell, but as far as we were aware, nothing was ever done, because it was the girl's mother.

If you think this situation is an aberration, think again. According to an article in the *Journal of the American Medical Association*, 30 percent of sexual abuse is performed by women.

Of the remaining 70 percent, 65 percent is inflicted by a non-biologically related male.[1] In other words, *not by dad!*

The majority of men are good, healthy, balanced, whole human beings—the vast majority. We forget that. Society's focus is on the perverted minority, and the rest of us allow ourselves to be defined in those terms.

The majority of men have no sexual intentions toward their children. The majority of men are not sexual predators. They love their sons and daughters. They want to stay married to their best friend and love her for life. That's the majority!

If you're not in that majority, if you feel you have it in you to cross the line with your kids, then you have to open up to a trusted friend or counselor who can keep you accountable. Bring it to light with people who won't condemn you but will help you. Bring it to light, because bad things that might have happened to you don't need to be repeated with your children. Take a chance. Talk to your wife. Be open, especially if you have been sexually abused yourself. If you have been violated, then statistically you are in danger of repeating history. *Don't!* It's time to break the cycle. It's time to get it right, for your children's children.

ENDNOTE

1. Sheridan Hill, "In Defense of Men," *Journal of the American Medical Association*, Dec. 2, 1998.

Your Daughter Will Marry a Man Like You

Listen to this: a daughter will marry a man like her dad.

Jessica went through a phase of saying, "When I grow up, Dad, can I marry you?" And I said, "Sure, honey, of course you can." The fact is, she will. Jessica will marry me, in one form or another.

At this point you're probably thinking about how you were before you became a Christian...or even how you are now! My daughter's going to choose a guy like me?! Yes, it's frightening, isn't it? It means that *if I want Jessica to marry an exceptional, above-average guy, then that's who I have to be.*

I want my daughter to approach her search for a husband with a level of expectation about his: behavior, emotional openness, emotional vulnerability, ability to say "thank you" and "I'm sorry," ability to articulate, communicate, share and be affectionate, loving and attentive, his inner strength, commitment, passion for life, and his pursuit of Christ.

I realized one day that my desire to grow and change as a man was no longer just to be a good husband to Beccy but also to model to our daughters, Jessica and Amy, how a good husband acts. I want them shooting for the top 5 to 10 percent.

Discipline — Pulling the Weeds

Discipline is not about physically abusing kids. It's about pulling the bad stuff out of a potentially beautiful garden.

Kids are great. Most human beings are great. But we're all great-great-grandchildren of Adam and, like our first ancestor, we have sin-driven character flaws that need weeding. Every person has areas in their soul that need addressing. If we do a good job of weeding our children when they're younger, they'll have far less trouble pulling the roots out for themselves when they're adults.

THE KEY WEEDS

Lack of common courtesy is a weed. So is *disrespect* and *ingratitude*. These all represent a failure to value others because of a failure in relationship with others.

Self-hatred is a tragic weed to see in anyone, especially a young person. It expresses itself through *lack of confidence, lack of self-respect*, and *lack of self-belief*.

These weeds form a vicious circle that feeds on itself. Lack of confidence and self-respect lead to poor performance, which creates even more grounds for insecurity as well as the hopelessness that results in lack of initiative.

The #1 weed of all, though, *is rebellion*. Rebellion is a spirit of witchcraft; its fruit is lawlessness and its ultimate manifestation is

The #1 weed of all, though, is rebellion.

anarchy. It works at every level of society, whether a nation, a neighborhood, or a family. If there's rebellion in the nation, the ultimate destination is anarchy. If there's rebellion in your family and you allow it to run its course, you're heading toward anarchy. So to combat chaos in your family, you need to attack the roots of rebellion.

RULES WITHOUT RELATIONSHIP LEAD TO REBELLION

If you apply rules but don't have a relationship with the person affected by those rules, rebellion will flourish. Appropriate discipline in the family has to be based on balanced relationships. Get the relationships right and the rules will work. Lawlessness will become lawfulness. Anarchy will become order.

Let me make a further point about society as a whole. Society can't impose order on its people when there's anarchy at the family level. Social problems are a symptom of the rebellion that exists in families. If you don't have appropriate discipline in families, it won't exist in society. Social anarchy starts with the destruction of discipline in the family home and the breakdown of the family unit. Fix the families, and society will take care of itself. Rebellion is the weed, so address the *root* issue: lack of family relationships.

The key person in the whole of that equation is the father. We, the dads, are the ones who can do this. We're one generation away from revival—or anarchy. We choose the destination for the next generation. We make the difference, by being what a dad is supposed to be: a consistent, loving, compassionate, balanced, forgiving man who is full of grace, wisdom, and knowledge.

Tall order? No. Just a lifetime pursuit.

Remember, once you start being a dad, you never stop.

The Keys to Family Discipline

There are times when your children won't like what you do or say or ask of them. That's part of the territory. If your relationship is firmly founded, though, don't worry. There will always be a tomorrow for you and your children.

Today, though, your family needs discipline and it has to originate from you, Dad. So now that we've discussed the weeds we want to root out, let's look at the simple "garden tools" you can use to bring discipline to your family.

1. Rules without relationship lead to rebellion.

   Have this headline written in your brain. It's the origin of so many discipline problems. When guys hear the phrase "tough love," a lot of men focus on the "tough" but forget the "love."

2. Before you discipline a child, you must first have shown the child and then have requested of the child.

   If you haven't told your child not to scratch the nice shiny side of your DVDs, it's an issue of instruction, not discipline. If you haven't shown and haven't requested, you can't discipline.

   Only discipline for rebellion—not lack of knowledge. This is very liberating. Men often wonder what issues or actions really require discipline. Before you react, ask yourself the following: "Is what they have done rebellious, or is it an issue for instruction? Have I clearly explained this situation before? Have I shown them what is expected?" If the answer is "Yes...but they've done it anyway," it is time for discipline.

3. Applaud in public; correct in private.

   You should always applaud in public, so your child gets used to being affirmed in the presence of others. It builds their public sense of self-esteem. Correction should be in private, though. If you have a house full of people, take the child into another room so he or she won't be humiliated in front of others.

   The right ratio: one correction for every seven-trillion cuddles and "I love yous." Your corrections should cause your children to question their specific actions, not question your love for them. Give them loads of evidence that you love them in spite of the really dumb thing they just did and that you have asked them not to do a hundred times before.

4. Physical punishment is only one of many ways to get the point across.

   Physical punishment is the last resort.

5. There's a big difference between discipline and beating.

6. There's a big difference between *loving* and *tolerating bad behavior.*

   You love your kids, but you don't have to put up with them acting like brats. Tolerating them behaving rudely or breaking things willfully isn't loving. In fact, it is the opposite. If you tolerate it, you are setting them up for a lifetime of unacceptable, immature behavior.

7. Correction when angry isn't discipline—it's reaction.

   If your children have made you angry, send them to their room for 10 minutes. The stewing will do them good. It will also give you and your wife time to regroup, discuss, and devise a plan to conquer the little rogue together!

Dad: The Enforcer!

A mother is a natural nurturer. A father is a natural disciplinarian. When a mother has to raise a child on her own, she loses the whole natural element of security and discipline in her family unit.

I am Beccy's greatest supporter. I am The Enforcer! Sure, she has to deal with day-to-day things, because that's the nature of our children's development and the way we've decided to raise our kids. But Beccy doesn't have to be The Enforcer.

As The Enforcer I will support every decision Beccy makes. In front of the kids I am unquestioning. If there's an issue, we will discuss it in the quiet of another room, but we will never discuss it in front of the kids. The Enforcer never questions! The Enforcer always backs up Mom's decision.

What if I think Beccy's decision is too extreme or reactionary? I won't discuss it in front of the kids. I'll say, "Honey, let's talk about it," and we'll go into another room.

When we've come to a decision, it's important that I don't come out and say, "This is what I've decided." Instead, Beccy is the one who comes out and says, "I've changed my mind. This is what I've decided to do now." That way her authority is affirmed, not eroded.

It works both ways: both of you should actively support each other in front of the kids. Don't let the children see you divided over fundamental things like discipline.

We haven't always been like that. I remember Beccy and I having an "exchange" and Jessica turned to her mother and asked, "How come you're always fighting with Daddy over things?"

What? Wake-up call! I thought, "That's really dangerous," so I went back and apologized to Beccy, in front of the kids. It made us instantly aware that our children are monitoring everything we say. The thing is, we weren't shouting. We were talking softly. But Jessica heard the firmness in our voices and interpreted it as a fight. Our child was aware of the intonation of every word we said.

So when it comes to the rules, I do not debate them with Beccy. I am The Enforcer. It's my job to *enforce* the rules we have agreed on, which, in turn, reflects the values we see as important. And Beccy is always my supporter when the roles are reversed.

The children must respect their mother — I enforce that rule.

The children must respect their mother—I *enforce* that rule. They must do what their mother asks, at once—I *enforce* that rule. Our kids will not throw tantrums—I enforce that rule.

Jessica has only ever thrown one tantrum. We dealt with it appropriately and it has never happened since—because The Enforcer didn't let her get away with it.

You get what you go for with kids.

Jessica has only ever run away from us in a parking lot once. We didn't laugh about it; we didn't think it was funny. We dealt with it straight away. We felt it was a big issue, because when we asked her to come back and she didn't, in a parking lot, on a road, it could have had dire consequences. So The Enforcer insisted that she come back.

And today we reap the benefits of it. Now she can run in a park for a million miles and when she's asked to come back, she does. No arguments, no tantrum, no debates; just sweet compliance.

It's not cute when a kid is running away from parents and laughing while they shout at the child to come back. That's not cute—that's rebellion. If Dad tolerates that, he's actually reinforcing the idea that rebellion's okay. So Dad has to become The Enforcer. The Enforcer does not tolerate rebellion.

Is The Enforcer sounding like a scary guy? Not scary, but real. Your kids will know that even in your guise as The Enforcer, you love them unconditionally. Unconditional love is not love without bound-aries. It's not love without discipline.

"My Dad loves me," they'll say, "so he gets me to obey the rules. He's The Enforcer!"

A MAN'S CHILDREN AND HIS GARDEN

BOTH REFLECT THE AMOUNT

OF WEEDING DONE DURING

THE GROWING SEASON.

Unknown

Thoughts on Discipline and Rewards

What does discipline look like in my house?

I do believe in a spank on the bottom. The bottom is this little fatty appendage with no nerve endings, yet it is somehow wonderfully connected to a child's memory! I *do not* believe in beating. I don't believe in inflicting meaningless violent harm on children. But correction— yes, I do believe in that based upon the clear instructions from the Word of God.

Physical punishment is not solely the domain of draconian child abusers. If it's done with love—and consistency—in a caring environment, physical discipline is a very effective way to enforce important rules and values.

Myth: Physical discipline is physical violence against a child and will shatter the child's view of the loving parent.

There's a whole gamut of difference between violence and a pat on the bottom.

Giving a child a tap on the leg with your hand or an inanimate object is our definition of physical discipline. It sends a message but it won't shatter a world view. Physically grabbing a child, shaking a child, and *beating* a child is violence. That's abuse.

Never spank your child while you are angry. This is when lines can be crossed.

If there's an issue you really believe calls for physical discipline but you're furious, put the child in another room for 10 minutes. Cool down and then deal with the issue.

I know there are people who want to redefine physical discipline as child abuse. I believe that's an overreaction by genuinely well-intentioned people, but I think they're playing right into the hands of a social strategy that undermines the family.

I would rather see a father coolly and calmly deal with a situation with physical discipline than watch another helpless single mother scream abuse in a shopping center because her child has refused to respond. One of these causes long-term damage—and it's not the tap on the bottom.

The Bible says you drive foolishness out with a rod. It really works. You cannot have a rational discussion with a 3 year old about the consequences of putting their hand on the "nice red fire."

They will not enter into a discussion on the gross pain the heater will inflict if they touch it. I don't want to wait until my child is burned to learn that lesson. Much better for him to learn that if he reaches for the heater, he'll get a little smack. He'll learn not to touch the heater, without getting burned. It's been proven for centuries: A child's bottom is connected to their memory.

A friend told me a story about his 8-year-old cousin running screaming through a Christmas party, chasing his 6-year-old sister with a 9" carving knife. He was seriously intent on stabbing her in the back. Emotionally, he was out of control. His mother grabbed his arm as he ran through the kitchen. She took the knife away and then she *discussed* it with him! She talked about how he would not feel like a valuable person if he hurt his sister, how this would not be a good feeling for him. I tell you, that is *not* a discussion to have with an 8 year old wielding a carving knife. The kid wasn't interested. The "discipline" of rational discussion had no impact but to bore him. He screamed, he yelled, and later they had to pull the kid off his sister as he beat her. What did the parents do? They *discussed* with him how he felt now that he had broken his sister's nose!

THE REWARDING ALTERNATIVE

There are definitely alternatives to smacking when it comes to disciplining your children. *The removal of privileges* is very effective. *Time out* works too, when the children are sent to their room for a short time.

But instead of just disciplining for the negative, *reward for the positive*. Reward positive behavior. Reward courtesy. Reward thoughtfulness. Reward politeness. Reward thankfulness. Reward compliance.

It's been proven for centuries: A child's bottom is connected to their memory.

Rewarding the positive activates the process of encouraging your child to grow in that area.

How to reward? Chocolates are good. An ice cream treat every now and again is too. Hop in the car and go for a drive with Dad. A big thank you. A cuddle. "Noah, I just want to thank you so much for being polite to your mother. I think it's just wonderful that you did that." Lots of positive caresses and positive touch. These are all part of the whole gamut of rewards.

If you make a big thing about these little rewards, they become big rewards—big affirmations, big cuddles, big kisses.

It's *rewarding to reward*, seeing the delight in their eyes because they've done well. They get so encouraged to do well again next time.

ABC, Consistently

Whether you're correcting or rewarding, the most important factor in family discipline is this: *consistency*. Be consistent about what you do and the behavior you reinforce. Your children should know what to expect from you.

Don't be moody in your discipline or your rules. A lot of parents let their emotional moods dictate the household discipline at any particular moment. So when they're upbeat, anything goes. When they're stressed, the kids are on eggshells.

Hey, being spontaneous is great during the fun times, but when it comes to discipline, Dad should be utterly, boringly predictable.

In summary, here are my ABCs:

AFFECTION—loads of it.

BOUNDARIES—the right from the wrong.

CONSISTENCY—the same message every day, in every way.

A + B + C = DISCIPLINE

This is a sample formula that works.

WORDS THAT WOUND

Do not verbally abuse children. I've heard it, and I think it's arguably worse than physically hurting your child.

The effects of verbally degrading or ridiculing children are very damaging and can last a lifetime. I've heard people ridicule their children, berate them, and mock them. People say: "Sticks and stones will break my bones but names will never hurt me." That's naive. Cuts heal; name calling scars for life!

When people talk to me about issues from their childhood, it's never about being taken into a private room and being given appropriate discipline to reinforce a loving verbal request. Instead, the things that haunt people from their early years are the terrible wounding words from angry people.

Please, be careful what you say to your children. All the guidelines we've set out in the last few chapters apply just as much to your tongue: about responding, not reacting; not rebuking in anger; being consistent; applauding in public, correcting in private; and balancing each correction with seven-trillion cuddles and "I love yous."

Honoring the Cofounder of your Family — Their Mother

This section of the book is very important to me. It's a footnote dedicated, with honor, to the wonderful women who fulfill our own lives and nurture our children.

Your wife is your best asset, your best friend, and your greatest companion. If she's not, your children will know it already. They will feel insecure and shaky, because Mom and Dad's relationship is not solid.

Every time you interact with your spouse, you are modeling marriage to your children. How you treat your wife, the mother of your daughter, is the way your daughter will grow up expecting to be treated by her husband.

Kiss their mother publicly, praise their mother publicly, esteem their mother publicly, so they will always speak well of you and their mother in private.

REAL GUYS LOVE THEIR WIVES

One passage of scripture that continues to challenge people in the area of marriage is from Paul's letter to the Ephesians: *Wives, submit to your husbands as to the Lord* (Ephesians 5:22).

The reason this causes so much trouble is that people—both men and women—neglect a verse that follows: *Husbands, love your wives, just as Christ loved the church...* (Ephesians 5:25).

Christ was a servant leader. Husbands must be the same for their wives. If you love your wife, you'll treat her better than you treat yourself. Christ was ready to die for His Church, and a husband should be prepared to die for his wife. Christ presented the Church blameless and without blemish. It's a husband's job to help his wife fulfill and attain everything she's supposed to become. You have to be preoccupied with her dreams, wishes, and desires. A man's role is to be a servant to his wife.

But there was never an issue about Christ being a weak leader. Christ was not a walkover. There was never a question about Christ being a real man. Nor was Christ abusive. He was a perfect servant, a perfect leader, a perfect man. Your job is to be a man who serves the woman he leads.

I have never met a balanced, well-adjusted woman who had a problem with that kind of relationship. Anything with two heads is a monster. Families aren't democracies. There is and always will be a leader in every situation.

The love of a serving, leading man will transform your wife into a loving, serving woman. And the outflow of your commitment to love your wife will transform your kids' world, too.

CHILDREN LOVE IT WHEN YOU LOVE THEIR MOM

"Ugh!"—that's what kids often say when they see Mom and Dad being affectionate. But they do really want to see a loving relationship. If they've seen Mom and Dad argue, they want to see them make up. If the disagreement was public, the making up should be public too, so that the children can see the act of reconciliation as well as the act of tension.

Loving your wife or focusing your attention on her is not an act of child neglect or rejection. Loving your wife is the best way to love your children. Ensuring that your marriage is healthy, strong, and long-lived is the most important thing you can do for your children.

In fact, I'd go so far as to say that the best time you can spend for your child...is alone on a date with your wife! If you're not getting the love renewal with your wife, if you're not filling up each other's emotional tanks, if you're not having sex for the reason behind the sex (the intimate connection of soul and spirit), then there's no glue. If there's no glue, your marriage will be shaky and so will your children.

DON'T STOP DATING

It's all about setting time aside for your wife, to let her know she's the center of your world.

There's a great book called *The Sensible Single Man's Guide to Women* which took the results of women's surveys and presented them in a very entertaining way.[1] It turns out that women enjoy a picnic rather than a romantic dinner. They would rather sit down with you in a quiet spot where it's just the two of you with time to talk.

My wife and I like going to the movies. We go, we hold hands, we have ice cream and popcorn. It costs 30 bucks, compared with 150 at a restaurant. It's what we liked to do before we got married and it's what we still like to do.

It's all about setting time aside for your wife, to let her know she's the center of your world.

Extravagant dating has its place, though. Once a year we'll blow 500 or 600 dollars on a very expensive restaurant and a nice hotel room. That's a lot of money, I know, but factored out over a year, it's only 10 dollars a week for a very important investment in our relationship.

It's all about setting time aside for your wife to let her know she's the center of your world. Flowers do it too—but not just because you've had an argument. Send a card. Leave a note. Do something totally unexpected, for no reason at all. Give her a journal to write her favorite thoughts, or tulip bulbs to plant for next spring beauty.

In all these ways it's important to communicate your love for your children's co-producer. I'm talking about making the strategic effort to send her the kind of message women respond to very strongly: "I'm preoccupied, honey. I'm preoccupied with *you*! All day long!"

Don't stop dating this wonderful woman just because you're married with children.

ENDNOTE

1. Searby, Charles & Allen, Richard *The Sensible Single Man's Guide to Women*, (Sydney Australia, Hoddler Headline, 2000).

Like Father, Like Son

If you are the father of sons, your boys will grow up either knowing how to treat a woman, or not knowing. It's up to you: the way you treat the #1 woman in their life, their mother.

Ian Woods, a great mentor in the area of family relationships for Beccy and me, has three boys who are all adults now and they still kiss their mother on the cheek "hello" and "goodbye" on every occasion. They defer to their mother. They're respectful to her. They stand until their mother is seated at the table. They open doors for her.

Where did they pick up these attributes that not only thrill their mom but also every woman they treat this way? It was modeled by their father. If your child does not say "thank you" for a meal that has been prepared or for a courtesy paid them, it's because you have not taught them how to respond to their mother. You may be the world's most gracious guy to the thousands of people you meet in business, but the model you set for your kids is the way you treat their mother. You reap what you sow.

You want your children to respect their mother? Then actively respect her yourself. Teach your children by your example. Our daughter thanks her mother for every meal she prepares. Why? Because I do. In fact, this goes back to the time when I noticed Jessica wasn't doing that. And do you know what else I noticed? I wasn't doing it! So instead of trying to teach my child what I wasn't doing, I started doing it. "Beccy, that was a fantastic dinner. Jessica, what did you think of dinner?" Jessica got the message—"Thanks, Mom. That was a great dinner"—and my child has been changed, because I changed.

PHYSICALLY AFFECTIONATE

I think your children need to see you being physically intimate with your wife. Now, unless you're being willfully perverse, I think you know what I mean by that...and what I don't mean by that. Society has tended to reduce physical intimacy to sexual contact, but that's because the only models we see of physical contact through the media are sexual. If that's all that's being modeled, that's all our kids will come to respect. They won't respect other people's boundaries and they'll have no concept of the whole spectrum of physical affection.

Give your children something more wholesome on which to model their view of physical affection. They need to see you're quite comfortable holding hands with their mother, kissing their mother, cuddling their mother. That is a very positive thing for children to see.

ALWAYS AVAILABLE, ALWAYS LISTEN

Ladies love to talk, so call your wife and talk to her. When she calls you at work or on the cell phone, understand that there's something she wants to say. Listen to those words. Stop what you're doing and hear her.

There's a certain length of conversation she wants. Give it to her. If you cut her off, you're just going to feel like a heel anyway, so you might as well just sit there and listen.

It's going to take, what, less than five minutes of your life? This is your best friend calling. Make her your priority. When everything else gets bumped by a meeting, your wife's call should be the one you take on your cell phone. Your wife should always be able to get straight past your secretary. She has to know she is the most important person in your life.

Your children are the same, of course, by extension. If your 15 year old knows you're available regardless of your schedule, she'll turn to you in a crisis. You know the kind: Her friend, Samantha, has bought the dress *she* was going to buy. If she knows she can bring this kind of problem to you 24/7, she'll do the same when she's in a real crisis, like being tempted into sexual intercourse, or when she just has questions about boys. She'll know that Daddy will be there for her. That's the kind of pattern we lay down in life. It's like a seed. Something significant starts small and it grows.

Seeds of Love, Not Bitterness

A few years ago, a friend and his wife separated. Individually they are two of the nicest people in the world. In fact, as a couple they were probably the most promising Christian ministers in our part of Australia. The tragedy is they just reached the point where they hated each other.

How did they get to this point where divorce was the only option because their relationship was broken beyond repair? They said it started with small things—seeds of bitterness, insidious comments to each other—all the way along in their marriage. They got to the point where they were overgrown with bitterness.

That's how it works in marriage, with the bad things and with the good. They start out as small seeds and grow into good things or bad things.

You Can Be a Fantastic Father

We humans are the only beings in all creation with the power to overcome instinct. Just because you have always reacted a certain way doesn't mean you have to continue that way. Just because things were done to you and you no longer trust people doesn't mean you have to spend your life living with lack of trust.

I'm not concerned with what your past is. I'm concerned with what your future is. We get so tied into our past that we think it has to be the script for our future. We don't have to let the past dictate our destiny! We can actively choose to let the baggage go and rewrite the script for our life.

The title of your new script can be your name with "Fantastic Father" written underneath it. Like I've said, it's as easy as ABC: *Affection*—you can do that; *Boundaries*—you can set them; *Consistency*—you can deliver it.

It's your destiny to become a whole man, a fantastic father. Destiny isn't about what you do; it's about who you become. When we leave our life, the legacy we leave isn't in the bricks and mortar; it's in the lives we've touched. Go ahead—touch the lives of your children so they won't have to "go looking for Dad." You'll be right there in the form of a great legacy of love and leadership.

Do it. Be the father you've always wanted to be and the man you are called to be.

Peace and grace to you and may God's love be with you...*always*.

IT IS EASIER FOR A FATHER

TO HAVE CHILDREN THAN

FOR CHILDREN TO HAVE

A REAL FATHER.

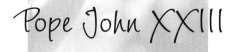

Pope John XXIII

ANY MAN CAN FATHER A CHILD,

BUT IT TAKES SOMEONE

SPECIAL TO BE A DAD!

Mark Twain

Resources

International Men's Network

Hundreds of practical teachings and instructions on DVD, CD, and MP3 available at www.imnonline.org.

Building Iron Men Network

A monthly men's discipleship program with DVD with study notes and audio CD for use in individual or group settings; available at www.imnonline.org.

Guy Thing Magazine

Free online magazine for men
www.guythingmag.org

Ed Cole Radio

All the MP3 teaching of Dr. Edwin Louis Cole – FREE
www.edcole.org

Focus on the Family

Great resources to help with everything from marriage to raising kids. Very practical and balanced material. www.family.org

Men's Leadership Ministries

This organization was founded by Steve Farrar and his books have greatly impacted my own life. www.stevefarrar.com

AUTHOR'S RECOMMENDED REFERENCE BOOKS

Maximized Manhood by Edwin Louis Cole

(The *best* men's book ever written, in my view. It turned my life around.)

Anchor Man by Steve Farrar

Bringing Up Boys by Dr. James Dobson

(Beccy found this book a great help with understanding Noah and the differences between raising boys and girls.)

Wild at Heart: Discovering the Secret of a Man's Soul
by John Eldredge (I wish I had written this one.)

The Five Love Languages by Gary Chapman
(Beccy said I had to read it.)

Raising a Modern-day Knight by Robert Lewis

(This book is a really great look at giving young men rites of passage.)

Author's Ministry

International Men's Network (IMN) exists to inspire all men to rise to a standard of manhood.

> ENCOURAGING them to excel in their roles as leaders, husbands, fathers, and friends.
>
> CHALLENGING them to be contributors to society and set an example based on a biblical value system that will benefit this generation and lay a solid foundation for the next.

For more information about the activities and resources of the International Men's Network, or if you would like to schedule Dr. John King as a keynote speaker for your conference or men's event please contact us at:

International Men's Network

PO Box 827
Roanoke, TX 76262
USA Telephone: 817-993-0047
Fax: 817-674-6100
E-mail: johnking@imnonline.org

Or visit our Website at www.imnonline.org

BUILDING IRON MEN
N E T W O R K

The *Building Iron Men Network* offers DVD video training resources for individuals, business, sporting, and faith-based organizations.

Every month Dr. John King and the men of the International Men's Network bring you the best in teaching that is designed to inspire and equip you to live as men of valor, men of courage, and men of purpose—to live as Iron Men in a spineless world.

Every month you will receive a DVD and audio CD of the teaching, along with study notes and a suggested reading guide. If this teaching is part of your organization's program you will also receive a license that allows you to duplicate and distribute FREE of charge the audio teaching to the men attending.

To learn more and to enroll, visit www.imnonline.org.

Additional copies of this book and other book titles from DESTINY IMAGE are available at your local bookstore.

Call toll-free: 1-800-722-6774.

Send a request for a catalog to:

Destiny Image® Publishers, Inc.

P.O. Box 310
Shippensburg, PA 17257-0310

"Speaking to the Purposes of God for This Generation and for the Generations to Come"

For a complete list of our titles, visit us at www.destinyimage.com